ALSO BY JEFFREY ROSEN

The Unwanted Gaze

The Naked Crowd

RANDOM HOUSE

NEW YORK

The Naked Crowd

RECLAIMING

SECURITY AND FREEDOM

IN AN ANXIOUS AGE

Jeffrey Rosen

Library of Congress Cataloging-in-Publication Data

Rosen, Jeffrey
The naked crowd: reclaiming security and freedom in an
anxious age / by Jeffrey Rosen.
p.   cm.
Includes bibliographical references and index.
ISBN 0-375-50800-7
1. Civil rights—United States.   2. National security—United States.
3. September 11 Terrorist Attacks, 2001.   4. War on Terrorism, 2001–
5. Terrorism—United States—Prevention.   I. Title.

JC599.U5R635 2004   323.44'8'0973—dc22   2003054808

Printed in the United States of America
on acid-free paper

Random House website address:
www.atrandom.com

246897531

FIRST EDITION

Book design by Barbara M. Bachman

For Christine

What marriage may be in the case of two persons of cultivated
faculties, identical in opinions and purposes, between whom
there exists that best kind of equality, similarity of powers and
capacities with reciprocal superiority in them—so that each
can enjoy the luxury of looking up to the other, and can have
alternately the pleasure of leading and of being led in
the path of development—I will not attempt to describe.

JOHN STUART MILL, *The Subjection of Women*

Contents

The Naked Crowd

The Naked Crowd

AFTER THE TERRORIST ATTACKS OF SEPTEMBER 11, 2001, officials at Orlando International Airport began testing a remarkable new security device. Let's call it the Naked Machine, for that's more or less what it is. A kind of electronic strip search, the Naked Machine bounces microwaves and millimeter waves off the human body. In addition to exposing any guns or other weapons that are concealed by clothing, the Naked Machine produces a three-dimensional naked image of everyone it scrutinizes.[1] Unlike the crude metal detectors used at airports today, the Naked Machine can detect ceramic and plastic as well as metal, allowing airport monitors to distinguish between lethal explosives and harmless nail clippers. The technologists who invented the Naked Machine hope that it will be deployed in the future not only at airports but also in schools, at public monuments, in federal buildings, and in prisons. Before we enter any vulnerable public space, the Naked Machine could strip us bare and confirm that we have nothing to hide.

The Naked Machine is a technology that promises a high

degree of security, but it demands a correspondingly high sacrifice of liberty and privacy, requiring all travelers to expose themselves nakedly, even though they raise no particular suspicions and pose no particular threats. Many people feel that this is a small price to pay in an age of terror: What's a moment or two of embarrassment if terrorists are thwarted as a result? But the Naked Machine doesn't have to be designed in a way that protects security at the cost of invading privacy. With a simple programming shift, researchers at the Pacific Northwest National Laboratory in Washington State have built a prototype of a redesigned Naked Machine that extracts the images of concealed objects and projects them onto a sexless mannequin.[2] The lurking image of the naked body is then scrambled into an unrecognizable and nondescript blob. (For most of us, this is an act of mercy.) This more discreet version of the Naked Machine—let's call it the Blob Machine—guarantees exactly the same amount of security without depriving liberty or invading privacy. Unlike the Naked Machine, the Blob Machine is a silver bullet technology that promises dramatic benefits without obvious costs; if it were deployed at airports, or perhaps even on subways and buses, the most scrupulous defenders of liberty and privacy could greet it with gratitude and relief.

For those who care about preserving both liberty and security, the choice between the Blob Machine and the Naked Machine might seem to be easy. But in presenting a hypothetical choice between the Naked Machine and the Blob Machine to groups of students and adults since 9/11, I've been struck by a surprising pattern: There are always some people who say they would prefer, at the airport, to go through the Naked Machine rather than the Blob Machine, even if the lines for each were equally long. When asked why, the people who choose the Naked Machine over the Blob Machine give a range of responses. Some say they are already searched so thoroughly at airports that they have abandoned all hope of privacy and don't mind the additional intrusion of being seen naked. Others say they're not embarrassed to be naked in front of strangers, adding that those who have nothing to hide should have nothing to fear. (A few are unapologetic exhibitionists.) Still others are concerned that the Blob Machine would be less accurate in identifying weapons than the Naked Machine, and they would prefer not to take chances. And in each group, there are some people who say they are so afraid of terrorism on airplanes that they would do anything possible to make themselves feel better, even if they understand, on some level, that their reaction is based on emotions rather than evidence. They describe a willingness to be electronically stripped by the Naked Machine as a ritualistic demonstration of their own purity and trustworthiness in much the same way that the religiously devout describe rituals of faith. They don't care, in other words, whether or not the Naked Machine makes them safer than the Blob Machine because they are more concerned about feeling safe than being safe.

In their willingness to choose a technology that threatens privacy without bringing more security, the people who prefer the Naked Machine to the Blob Machine are representative of an important strain in public opinion as a whole. It has become a cliché to say that everything changed after 9/11; but the cliché, on so many levels, is wrong. Before and after 9/11, when presented with images of remote but terrifying events, groups of people have tended to be moved by emotions rather than arguments, and this has led them to act in ways that sociologists and psychologists have associated with the behavior of crowds. Crowds tend to personalize risk and exaggerate the probability of its recurrence. They demand high levels of security while assigning less weight to more abstract values like liberty and privacy. Like the fearful people who prefer the Naked Machine, the public is sometimes more concerned about feeling safe than being safe. And it has little patience for evaluating the complicated choices that are necessary to ensure that laws and technologies are designed in ways that protect liberty and security at the same time.

This book began as an attempt to respond to a challenge posed by my friend Lawrence Lessig, who teaches at Stanford Law School and is the most creative and provocative philosopher of cyberspace. We were participating in a panel discussion about technologies of security, and I expressed skepticism about the proliferation of surveillance cameras in Britain, arguing that the cameras posed grave threats to privacy even though the British government's own studies had found that they resulted in no measurable decrease in terrorism or crime.[3] Lessig politely but firmly called me a Luddite. These technologies will proliferate whether we like it or not, he said, and he encouraged me to think about ways of designing the technologies and constructing legal regulations in ways that might protect liberty and security at the same time. In the course of trying to answer Lessig's challenge, I've become convinced that it is indeed possible, in theory, to design technologies and laws that protect both liberty and security. Unlike civil libertarians such as Alan Dershowitz[4] and Steven Brill,[5] who, in the wake of 9/11, uncritically embraced technologies such as national ID cards without acknowledging the complicated range of choices they pose, I've been persuaded that there are well-designed and badly designed architectures of identification, surveillance, and data mining, and the decision to accept or resist them should be guided by the details of the design and the values that constrain the designers.

As the response to the Naked Machine shows, however, it's also hard to be optimistic, in an anxious age, that Western democracies will, in fact, adopt these well-designed laws and technologies, rather than settling for poorly designed alternatives. In the pages that follow, I will explore the reasons why the public may not demand laws and technologies that protect liberty and security, and why the legislatures may not require them, the courts may not refine them, and the technologists may not supply them on their own. I will examine the social as well as technological reasons why the risk-averse democracies of the West continue to demand ever-increasing levels of surveillance and exposure in a search for an illusory and emotional feeling of security. The result is the peculiar ordeal of living in the Naked Crowd, whose vulnerabilities and anxieties I will attempt to describe. In the epilogue, I will try to imagine scenarios that might encourage the adoption of well-designed laws and technologies, and to evaluate models that those laws and technologies might follow. But my primary goal is to describe the challenge, rather than presuming to suggest that there are easy solutions: In societies ruled by public opinion, the excesses of public opinion can't be easily overcome.

By focusing on the emotionalism of some of the public responses to fears of terror, I don't mean in any way to deny or minimize the gravity of the new threats we face. At the beginning of the twenty-first century, the dangers of terrorist attacks on the Western democracies are clear, present, and deadly serious, and the need for effective responses to these dangers should be our highest priority of national security. My concern, however, is that the technologies and laws demanded by a fearful public often have no connection to the practical realities of the threats that confront us. We run the risk, therefore, of constructing vast but ineffective architectures of surveillance and identification that threaten the liberty and privacy of innocent citizens without protecting us from terrorism. And although individuals should be free, in a pluralistic society, to trade liberty and privacy for higher levels of security, it's hard to defend government policies that require the surrender of liberty and privacy without bringing demonstrable security benefits. These feel-good laws and technologies may also distract the government from the focused intelligence gathering that has proven to be the most successful response to terrorism in the past.

This is a book about the anxieties of the Naked Crowd in an age of terror; and in this sense, it is also a book about our anxieties about identity at the beginning of the twenty-first century. Now that we can no longer rely on the traditional markers of identity—such as clothes or family or religion—to make judgments about whether or not strangers in the crowd pose risks to our security, fearful citizens are turning instead to technologies of identification and risk management. The interest after 9/11 in surveillance cameras, data-profiling systems at airports, integrated databases of personal information, and biometric identification systems is one sign of our fears and confusion about whom to trust. But the question of whether trust is possible in a society of strangers is not unique to 9/11: It has been an enduring social challenge of the modern era. As traditional communities, social hierarchies, and natural systems of surveillance broke down in the twentieth century, the question of trust became especially acute.[6] Many of the surveillance technologies that arose in the private sector in the second half of the twentieth century were designed to verify personal identity and to distinguish between trustworthy and untrustworthy consumers. In short, the search for technologies that might predict future behavior and put people in conveniently ranked categories predated our fears of terrorism; as we will see, many of the same risk-profiling technologies that were used before 9/11 to classify and monitor customers on Amazon.com were deployed after 9/11 to classify and monitor potential terrorists.

The sociologist Anthony Giddens has described modernity as a "risk culture,"[7] in which individuals, no longer able to rely on customary sources of identity such as tradition and family and religion, must define themselves each day from an infinite variety of lifestyle choices. In an individualistic society, the effort to calculate risk becomes an obsessive preoccupation, not because individuals face more life-threatening dangers than in the past—in the age of antibiotics, we face fewer—but because the need to anticipate the future becomes especially pressing in a world where fewer aspects of our lives follow a predestined course. In an uncertain world, in which the status of individuals is constantly shifting, people find it increasingly difficult to live on what Giddens calls "automatic pilot."[8] Public discourse becomes addicted to predicting the future: As the proliferation of pundits, risk profilers, and futurologists suggests, people are desperate for guidance about how to plot their life choices from a bewildering variety of options. The constant calculation of future risks becomes a psychological crutch and a market imperative: Witness the wave of books with "Future" in the title, from *Future Shock* to *The Future of Work* (or *Freedom* or *Ideas,* or what have you). "A significant part of expert thinking and public discourse today is made up of *risk profiling*—analysis of what, in the current state of knowledge and in current conditions, is the distribution of risks in given milieux of action," Giddens writes. "Since what is 'current' in each of these respects is constantly subject to change, such profiles have to be chronically revised and updated."[9] In this sense, America's preoccupation with risk transcends the particular (and undeniably real) threats we now face. Previous ages have been menaced by catastrophes, plagues, and dangerous fanatics. Instead, our current preoccupation with risks reflects the peculiar malleability of modern identity: An effort to anticipate risks is a self-defense mechanism in a world where we are forced increasingly to make judgments about the trustworthiness of those we will never meet face-to-face.

In addition to embracing technologies of identification that purport to tell them whom to trust, citizens also face increasing pressure to expose personal information, in order to prove that they have nothing to hide. Crowds react to individuals in the same emotional terms that they react to remote threats; and as individuals on the Internet are increasingly exposed to vast audiences of strangers, many find it hard to resist the temptation to strip themselves bare in the hope of attracting the attention and winning the trust of a virtual audience. Celebrities have long been familiar with the public pressure to reveal personal information: The illusion of familiarity that celebrity creates leads to growing demands that celebrities open up their personal lives, in order to sustain a sense of emotional connection with their unseen audience. In the age of the Internet, private citizens are experiencing similar pressure to expose themselves in the manner of celebrities. In the Naked Crowd, citizens who resist the overwhelming social pressure to reveal personal information to prove their trustworthiness are suspected of being potential terrorists, elitists, or, worst of all, nobodies.

The sociologist Thomas Mathiesen has contrasted Michel Foucault's Panopticon—a surveillance house in which the few watched the many—with what he calls the "Synopticon" created by modern television, in which the many watch the few.[10] But in the age of the Internet, we are experiencing something that might be called the "Omnipticon," in which the many are watching the many, even though no one knows precisely who is watching or being watched at any given time. The technology now exists to bring about the fulfillment of a particular kind of dystopia, where no aspects of life are immune from the relentless scrutiny of public opinion, and where the public's lack of tolerance for individuality and eccentricity results in a suffocating and pervasive social conformity. "At present individuals are lost in the crowd," John Stuart Mill wrote in the nineteenth century. "In politics it is almost a triviality to say that public opinion now rules the world." Mill was equally concerned that public opinion would infiltrate the "moral and social relations of private life," as "inhabitants of distant places," increasingly brought into "personal contact" by "improvements in the means of communication," would increasingly "read the same things, listen to the same things, see the same things, go to the same places, have their hopes and fears directed to the same objects, have the same rights and liberties, and the same means of asserting them."[11]

In the twenty-first century, changes in politics and technology have dramatically exacerbated the tyranny of public opinion. As traditional authorities continue to decline, and public opinion becomes the only judgment that can command respect and deference, more and more aspects of our public and private lives become infiltrated by the logic of polls, evaluations, focus groups, and democratic accountability. Teachers are evaluated by their students and CEOs by their employees. Buyers and sellers evaluate one another on eBay and Amazon.com, and the telephone company asks customers to assess and rank even the most mundane interactions with sales representatives as a reminder that every opinion matters and must be counted. As technologies make it possible for more and more aspects of our lives to be observed by strangers, they also ensure that more and more aspects of our lives will be evaluated by strangers. In the past, it was only unusually interesting people—celebrities, crime victims, or politicians—who had to worry about the face they presented to large and unseen audiences. But in the age of the Omnipticon, no individual is immune from the pitiless and unblinking gaze of the crowd, and all of us are susceptible to its fickle emotions—including anxiety, jealousy, and fear.

The excesses of the Naked Crowd were brought into sharp relief by the terrorist attacks of 9/11; but they are hardly a new phenomenon. In *The Crowd,* a classic nineteenth-century study of the popular mind, Gustave Le Bon argued that impulsiveness, irritability, and absence of critical spirit are "the special characteristic of crowds."[12] As a result, he concluded, the sentiments of crowds tend to be simplistic, exaggerated, and over-confident. Crowds are moved by images rather than arguments, he wrote, and the images most likely to impress a crowd are the most dramatic and therefore the least typical—great crimes, for example, or great miracles or disasters. But because crowds are incapable of reasoning, they have trouble distinguishing im-probable events, which tend to be the most memorable, from mundane events, which are more likely to repeat themselves. "A hundred petty crimes or petty accidents will not strike the imagination of crowds in the least, whereas a single great crime or a single great accident will profoundly impress them, even though the results be infinitely less disastrous than those of the hundred small accidents put together," Le Bon observed.[13] For example, a flu epidemic that killed 5,000 people in Paris made little impression on the popular imagination, because it was re-ported only in dry statistics that emerged week by week in the newspapers, while a visually memorable accident, such as the fall of the Eiffel Tower, would have made an immense impres-sion, even if it had killed fewer people. For all these reasons, Le Bon concluded, individuals act and feel very differently in crowds than when they are isolated from each other, and are es-pecially susceptible to irrational and contagious epidemics of fear.

Le Bon, it must be said, was a sexist and racist (and not only by our own more exacting standards); and his politically incor-rect generalizations have not always withstood the test of time. "Crowds are everywhere distinguished by feminine characteris-tics, but Latin crowds are the most feminine of all," he wrote.[14] Nevertheless, his insights about the tendency of crowds to be moved by images and emotions rather than arguments and analysis were confirmed during the twentieth century by more empirical behavioral economists and social psychologists, who resisted calling the public irrational but emphasized its "quasi-rationality"[15] or "bounded rationality"[16] in evaluating remote but frightening risks. These scholars found that people are vulnerable to systematic errors and biases in judgment; as a result, they have difficulty appraising the probability of especially frightening threats because of their tendency to make judgments about risk based on emotional intuitions about whether something is good or bad, rather than on a dispassionate calculation of costs and benefits. Groups of people also tend to fixate on the hazards that catch their attention, which means those that are easiest to imagine and recall. A single memorable image—of the World Trade Center collapsing, for example—will crowd out less visually dramatic risks in the public mind, and will lead people wrongly to imagine that they are more likely to be victims of terrorism than of mundane risks, like heart disease. Although mental shortcuts can work relatively well in some circumstances,[17] they can also create anxiety and panic that are disproportionate to the threat at hand.

Because people fear risks that produce memorable images above all, the psychology of fear is driven inextricably by images of terror transmitted by the media. In this sense, the growth of the Internet and 24/7 cable TV stations has exacerbated the biases and errors of judgment to which the public is vulnerable. After World War I, in his classic study of public opinion, Walter Lippmann pointed to the growth of motion pictures and newspapers, which created an increasing gap between the simplistic images in people's heads and the complicated reality of the remote threats that confronted American democracy. "The only feeling that anyone can have about an event he does not experience is the feeling aroused by his mental image of that event,"[18] Lippmann recognized, and as Americans increasingly faced threats far removed from their personal experience, the images that engaged them were likely to come from movies, radio, and newspapers. This created a new problem for democracy—"the problem which arises because the pictures inside people's heads do not automatically correspond with the world outside."[19]

In absorbing images from movies and newspapers, Lippmann worried, people were too impatient to make reliable judgments about complicated threats involving war and foreign affairs. "The truth about distant or complex matters is not self-evident, and the machinery for assembling information is technical and expensive," he wrote.[20] Besides, citizens in a modern democracy are not very good at absorbing complicated information from the media: Because of our short attention spans, we tend to simplify and generalize, reducing unfamiliar people and events to crude and easily intelligible stereotypes. Instead of imaginatively projecting ourselves into events that are remote from our daily experience, we selfishly try to relate these events to our own parochial concerns. "In almost every story that catches our attention we become a character and act out the role with pantomime of our own," Lippmann wrote. Instead of taking our "personal problems as partial samples of the greater environment," we instead reconfigure "stories of the greater environment as a mimic enlargement of [our] private life."[21] As a result, "self-centered" public opinion is likely to exaggerate the individual risk posed by remote events and to undervalue common interests such as liberty and privacy.

Since Lippmann wrote, the gap between the "pictures in our heads" and the reality of the threats that menace us has expanded dramatically because of the growth of new media. In *The Image,* written at the beginning of the 1960s, Daniel Boorstin explored the way the "Graphic Revolution"[22]—by which he meant the explosion of television as well as movies, newspapers, and magazines—had transformed the way Americans related to political leaders and to public affairs in general. The need to fill empty space on television and in magazines brought with it irresistible demands for the manufacturing of "pseudo-events"—that is, events created for the sole purpose of producing memorable images that could then be reported and consumed. Pseudo-events were distinctive, vivid, and easier to grasp than reality itself: Whether they were believable and memorable was more important than whether they were true.

In the 1990s, the proliferation of new media such as the Web and cable TV expanded the amount of empty airtime and exacerbated the demand for pseudo-events that would catch the public's attention in an increasingly fractured and competitive marketplace. Stations like FOX News and CNN converted themselves into twenty-four-hour purveyors of alarm, with shrieking banners running like stock tickers along the bottom of the screen, exaggerating the latest threat in the most lurid terms. ("Chilling chatter," read the banners on the first anniversary of 9/11, as the government reported intercepted messages from terrorists purportedly planning a new attack abroad.) These stations had a commercial incentive to exaggerate the risks posed by low-probability, randomly distributed threats, in order to convey the impression that everyone was at risk and therefore catch the attention of an easily distracted audience. But there are tangible effects to this brazen fear-mongering: When the Department of Homeland Security put the nation on a Level Orange alert for an imminent terrorist attack, there was a run at malls across America on duct tape and plastic sheeting, as people rushed to insulate their houses against a hypothetical chemical attack that never materialized.

The vicious cycle at this point should be clear. The public fixates on low-probability but highly terrifying risks because of dramatic images it absorbs from television and the Internet, which in turn have an incentive further to exaggerate the probability of the same remote risks in the hope of sustaining the attention of the public. This cycle fuels a demand for draconian and symbolic but often poorly designed laws and technologies of surveillance and exposure to eliminate the risks that are, by their nature, difficult to reduce. The demand for these ineffective and invasive laws and technologies is made even worse by the fact that the public tends to conceive of risks as an all-or-nothing affair: It mistakenly believes that a hazard is either dangerous or safe without recognizing the possibility of a middle ground. Many people embrace what W. Kip Viscusi of Harvard Law School has called a "zero risk" mentality, naively believing that it is possible to eliminate risks that can never entirely be eliminated.[23] This only increases the demand for showy safety rituals that are designed more to commemorate the last dramatic threat than to anticipate the next one.

It's possible, as the Blob Machine shows, to design laws and technologies that protect liberty and security, striking a more effective balance between exposure and concealment. But it's also hard to be optimistic that these laws and technologies will actually be adopted. The choices among them are complicated and the crowd's attention span is short. Moreover, there is no obvious political constituency for a reasonable balance between liberty and security. Our civic debate is polarized between technopositivists, who greet every proposed expansion in surveillance power with uncritical enthusiasm, and principled Luddites, who are fighting a doomed battle to resist technologies that will proliferate whether we like them or not. And rather than trying to ensure that these laws and technologies are designed well rather than poorly, even the self-styled pragmatists in the debate allow their judgment to be distorted by hyperbole and fear. "It stands to reason that our civil liberties will be curtailed" after September 11, wrote Judge Richard Posner soon after the attacks. "They should be curtailed, to the extent that the benefits in greater security outweigh the costs in reduced liberty. All that can reasonably be asked of the responsible legislative and judicial officials is that they weigh the costs as carefully as the benefits."[24] But this careful weighing of costs and benefits is precisely what legislators and judges have proved, in times of crisis, to be incapable of sustaining.

Why should we care about the emotionalism of the Naked Crowd? If citizens want to strip themselves naked at the airport because the ritual makes them feel better without making them safer than a less intrusive alternative, why should anyone else object? Of course, individual citizens should be free to surrender their own privacy in exchange for a feeling of security, as long as their choices are not imposed on anyone else. But when the government adopts vast technologies of surveillance and classification, Western democracies may slowly be transformed in ways that we are only beginning to understand. It may be worth imagining some of the social and individual costs of badly designed technologies and laws, in order to frame the debate about how to design them better.

As the government collects and stores more and more personal information about citizens in what Daniel Solove has called "digital dossiers,"[25] there is, first of all, the danger of the "Googleization" of identity—a phenomenon that could allow government agents to single out any individual from the crowd and reconstruct his or her movements, purchases, reading habits, and even private conversations for any period of time. Google, of course, is the Internet search engine that allows any citizen to punch in the name of any other citizen and instantly retrieve information about him or her that has appeared in cyberspace. It is one of the many technologies of identification that help us to acquire information about strangers and new acquaintances in deciding whom to trust, a substitute for more traditional ways of assessing someone's reputation, such as gossip or face-to-face judgments about character. Because Google retrieves isolated bits of personal information, a Google search inevitably runs the risk of confusing information with knowledge and of judging us out of context.

After being set up on a blind date, for example, a friend of mine ran a Google search and discovered that her prospective partner had been described in an article for an on-line magazine as one of the ten worst dates of all time; the article included intimate details about his sexual equipment and performance that she was unable to banish from her mind during their first—and only—dinner. These are the sorts of details, of course, that friends often exchange in informal gossip networks. The difference now is that the most intimate personal information is often recorded indelibly and can be retrieved with chilling efficiency by strangers around the globe.

As the government begins to use Google-like technologies of data mining and data profiling to judge people out of context, the consequences can be far more severe than embarrassment. Roger Clarke has used the term "dataveillance" to refer to the "systematic use of personal data systems in the investigation or monitoring of the actions or communications of one or more persons."[26] Clarke distinguishes between "personal dataveillance" of previously identified individuals and the "mass dataveillance" of groups of people. Personal dataveillance tends to be used for investigation and mass dataveillance for risk prediction; and both technologies present distinct costs and benefits.

Personal dataveillance—designed to collect information about individuals who have been identified in advance as suspicious—can be usefully deployed to catch the most serious criminals or to prevent the most serious crimes. In the fall of 2002, for example, the suburbs of Washington, D.C., were terrorized by two snipers who killed several people before being caught by the police. Although the risk of being killed by snipers was far lower than the risk of being killed in a car accident, the crime was so visible, and the TV images it produced were so dramatic, that otherwise rational citizens could be seen sprinting hysterically from their cars to the mall in a zigzag pattern, to avoid what they imagined were the sniper's crosshairs. The alleged snipers turned out to be an unemployed man who was traveling with a teenage Jamaican accomplice; they were caught, in the end, because one boasted to a priest about having committed a murder in Alabama. Based on this human tip, the police were able to engage in a form of personal dataveillance, connecting a fingerprint found at the Alabama crime scene with one stored in an Immigration and Naturalization Service database. They were then able to identify the sniper's accomplice and to track down his license plate number. This combination of old-fashioned police work and cross-referencing of criminal databases made fools of the criminal profilers and "forensic psychologists"[27] who filled weeks of airtime predicting that the sniper was an angry white man in his thirties who drove a white van. But the sharing of information about serious crimes among several government agencies was a defensible use of database technology: It allowed the identification of a serious criminal with no tangible threat to the privacy of innocent citizens.

When applied by the state on a broad scale, however, personal dataveillance can run the risk of judging people out of context, leading to arrests based on mistaken identity. For example, an FBI watch list widely circulated to private employers was riddled with inaccuracies, misspellings, and people who had been wrongly identified as terrorists. Many of these innocent victims were repeatedly stopped at the airport, and found it very difficult to clear their names once they had been tagged as suspicious in computer databases.[28] Other troubling cases in America after 9/11 involved immigrants who were arrested and detained for months based on snippets of circumstantial evidence suggesting that they fit a terrorist profile but who later turned out not to be terrorists. A man named Hady Hassan Omar was arrested on September 12 and detained for seventy-three days after he bought a one-way airline ticket on the same

Kinko's computer used by one of the 9/11 hijackers. An Egyptian named Osama Elfar was locked up for more than two months because he had attended a Florida flight school and worked as a mechanic for an airline in St. Louis. A gas station attendant from Pakistan was denied bail in Miami after being arrested because he stood in line to renew a driver's license a few minutes ahead of Mohammad Atta. An Egyptian student named Abdallah Higazy, who had been staying in a hotel near the World Trade Center on 9/11, was put in solitary confinement after FBI agents accused him of using a ground-to-air radio to transmit information to the terrorists. Only after another guest showed up to claim the radio were the charges dropped. Although these immigrants eventually had a chance to prove they weren't terrorists, many were later deported for having committed low-level crimes that had nothing to do with terrorism. Of the 130 Pakistanis seized after 9/11, 110 were convicted of immigration violations and 22 were convicted of robbery, credit card fraud, or drug possession. None was linked to the 9/11 attacks. A report by the inspector general of the Justice Department found that few of the 762 illegal immigrants arrested in the wake of 9/11 had obvious connections to terrorism. This pattern of misidentifying people as serious criminals and then punishing them for low-level offenses is typical of personal dataveillance, which gives the state tremendous discretion to single out individuals from the crowd and then to punish them for trivial crimes that are far easier to detect.

By contrast, mass dataveillance—which involves scanning the personal data of millions of citizens who have not been identified as suspicious in the hope of preventing terrorism before it occurs—poses very different dangers. These dangers are by no means new: In some ways, mass dataveillance looks very much like the general warrants that the framers of the Fourth Amendment to the Constitution were determined to prohibit. General warrants allowed the agents of King George III to break into any citizen's home and rifle through his or her private papers in a fishing expedition for evidence of disloyalty to the Crown. In the course of fishing for unspecified evidence of guilt, these general searches ran the risk of exposing a great deal of innocent but embarrassing private information—from personal diaries to private letters—to public view. Because the invasiveness of the search was so vastly out of proportion to the unspecified crimes that it might detect, the framers of the Fourth Amendment to the Constitution forbade general warrants and insisted that magistrates couldn't issue warrants without probable cause to suspect wrongdoing and without "particularly describing the place to be searched, and the persons or things to be seized."

Mass dataveillance, like general warrants, allows the government to scan a great deal of innocent information in the course of fishing for signs of guilt. And in the process, it threatens both privacy and equality, and diverts government resources away from more effective responses to terrorism. First consider privacy. One reason that the framers of the Fourth Amendment feared general warrants was the risk of blackmail and politically motivated retaliations against opponents of the government. Although this sort of abuse of power is thankfully harder to conceal in a more transparent age, it was only a generation ago that President Richard Nixon engaged in similar abuses, monitoring the private activities of antiwar protesters and vindictively prosecuting them for low-level tax offenses. In an age when the personal data of far greater numbers of citizens are analyzed by the government in personally identifiable ways, it's not wrong to fear versions of the Nixon effect on a broader scale. Moreover, the very existence of personally identifiable dossiers would be a temptation to those who wished us ill in the private sphere: As those who have endured messy divorces can attest, vindictive spouses are all too happy to fish for embarrassing personal information and to expose it to the world.

If technology and law are allowed to erode the old barriers that prevent government from searching citizens at random and prosecuting them for the most minor infractions of the law, many more citizens will experience the sense of indignation at living in a zero-tolerance society—an experience that before 9/11 was limited largely to citizens in minority communities. A zero-tolerance society should be distinguished from one that uses the prosecution of low-level crimes to prevent more serious crimes. In 1982, James Q. Wilson and George Kelling published a celebrated article called "Broken Windows" in *The Atlantic Monthly,* which argued that policing lower-level public disorders—loitering, drug use, gang activity, and public drinking—best diminished the fear and social disorder that allowed more serious crimes to flourish. But broken-windows policing was not based on the principle of zero tolerance, which advocates mass arrests for low-level crimes on the theory that some turnstile jumpers may turn out to be wanted for more serious crimes. The broken-windows approach instead urged cities to use quality-of-life offenses to increase police discretion, not to eliminate it. By allowing police to choose among a wide variety of legal and nonlegal sanctions for public disorders—from informal warnings to formal citations—the broken-windows policy viewed arrest as a last resort.

By contrast, when the broken-windows approach morphed into zero-tolerance policing, the minority community in New York rioted in the streets because people began to feel as though they were living in a police state. It was the zero-tolerance approach that led to undercover operations like Operation Condor, during which an officer shot Patrick Dorismond in the course of approaching him to buy marijuana that he turned out not to possess. Under Operation Condor, narcotics officers volunteered to work overtime to arrest people for minor crimes, such as smoking marijuana and trespassing. Operation Condor drove low-level drug-trafficking indoors, but it had little impact on the homicide rate, which actually increased, or on the rate of narcotic-felony arrests, which decreased by 9 percent. In other words, the zero-tolerance thesis— that turnstile jumpers often turn out, under investigation, to be carrying illegal guns—proves, after a certain point, to be wrong: Many pot smokers are guilty of nothing more than smoking pot. The experience of being accountable to the police for offenses so trivial that no one expects to be prosecuted made minority citizens take to the streets in protest. And in a zero-tolerance society in which all of our personal data were transparent to the government, it's not hard to imagine broader groups of citizens being moved to similar protests against what they perceived to be the inordinate power of a police state.

Because they are searching for needles in haystacks, the new technologies of mass dataveillance also run the risk of generating a very high number of "false positives"—alerts in which innocent citizens are misidentified as potential terrorists. (For a statistical illustration of why data-mining systems are not very good at picking very few individuals out of very large crowds, please see chapter 3.) Anyone who has been taken aside repeatedly for special searches on a particular airline will recognize the feeling of indignity and helplessness that results from being flagged as a threat in a computer database without knowing why or even having the power to confirm or deny that a blacklist actually exists. The chief architect at Microsoft described these feelings after being wrongly flagged for an airport search by the Computer Assisted Passenger Profiling System, or CAPPS, because he had trained for a pilot's license and bought a one-way ticket: "I suddenly felt as if in the grip of a giant vise, a terrible feeling I had last experienced as a teenager before fleeing Communist Hungary. . . . My friends may suspect I am suffering from some Hungarian Refugee Syndrome, which makes me overly sensitive to perfectly reasonable intrusions by the state. I try to explain: The communism I had fled was hardly traumatic or violent. One aspect of the horrible vise was the constant minor humiliations I had to suffer, such as interaction with the block warden, the party overlord of a block of houses, who had to give his assent to all matters tiny or grand, including travel. On this Friday in the United States, I was being singled out for an unusual and humiliating search. . . . So I did what I had done 30 years ago: I chose to be humiliated just so I could reach my goal."[29] Of course, the indignity that the Microsoft architect suffered in Communist Hungary was very different from the indignity that he suffered in the United States, but the sense of being wrongly identified on the basis of secret information that the government refuses to disclose is one that could well infuriate Americans if this kind of profiling becomes widespread.

Mass dataveillance threatens us with more than embarrassment and invasions of privacy: It also threatens our values of equality in ways that could transform the relationship between citizens and their government. Risk profiles ensure that different groups of individuals are treated differently in the future based on their behavior in the past. As the temptation to use profiling technology expands, citizens, in all of their interactions with the government, could be treated differently based on the level of trustworthiness they have been assigned by a computer search. In this sense, risk profiles are technologies of classification and exclusion, limiting people's opportunities and stifling their power to define themselves. "[R]educing the issue to one of 'privacy' simply deflects attention from . . . a social situation in which electronic languages are permitted to define us and channel our social participation," David Lyon has written. "[T]he language of surveillance all too often classifies, divides, and excludes."[30]

Classification and exclusion are already common in the consumer sphere, in which technologies of customer relations management are designed to put customers in separate categories based on their perceived value to the company. When the same technologies are applied in the civic sphere, however, they result in different citizens being put in different risk categories based on the threat they are perceived to pose to the state. In this sense, risk profiles extend harms similar to those imposed by racial profiling across society as a whole, creating electronic layers of second-class citizenship that determine who is singled out for special suspicion by state officials. They represent what

Lyon calls a technology of "social sorting" and "digital dis-crimination."[31] Individuals who are classified as especially high risk are likely to experience a sense of helplessness at their in-ability to confront the unknown accusations that dog them and a constant sense of having to prove their innocence in the face of a presumption of guilt.

There is a final danger of poorly designed technologies that make us feel safer without actually increasing our security: They may divert the government's resources and distract its at-tention from developing more effective responses to terrorism—responses that might actually save lives rather than temporarily ease anxieties. In airports, for example, human intelligence has proved far more effective than machines. El Al, the national airline of Israel, is famous for the zeal of its human security guards, who ask passengers where they are going, where they have come from, why they want to visit Israel, and whom they plan to see. The guards are trained to look for changes in facial expression or body language that might indicate nervousness, and are subject to elaborate simulation exercises that test their ability to pick suspicious travelers out of the crowd. Unlike CAPPS, a data-mining program that tries to predict who will be a terrorist, El Al tries only to determine whether a particular passenger poses a serious risk after he or she has been ques-tioned by a human security guard trained in psychological analysis.[32] Relying on the kind of visual profiles that Americans reject as a violation of equality, El Al screeners tend to single out Arabic-looking men, women traveling alone, and "shabbily dressed" people.[33] This crude visual profiling proved effective in 1986, when El Al officials prevented the bombing of a flight from London to Tel Aviv by focusing on a pregnant Irish woman who was traveling alone. Faced with additional questions, the woman admitted she was engaged to a Palestinian man, the father of her unborn child, who had packed a box of presents for her to carry to his family in the West Bank; on inspection, the bag turned out to contain explosives.[34]

El Al has been similarly effective in using behavioral profiling, focusing on passengers who seem unusually nervous or anxious. In a more recent case, El Al screeners apprehended a German criminal whose ticket had been purchased by a Palestinian terrorist group that had paid him $5,000 to carry what he thought were drugs. When the German couldn't explain why he was taking the trip or who had bought his ticket, security officers opened his bags and found hidden explosives.[35] After being trained in techniques of psychological profiling, El Al screeners must pass at least 150 security checks a year, including efforts by members of the Mossad, Israel's CIA, to test their human intelligence abilities by imitating passengers who offer incongruous stories. Instead of relying on computer algorithms, the Israelis recognize that there is no substitute for face-to-face human discretion.

IF PROPERLY DESIGNED to guarantee liberty and privacy as well as security, there is no reason that these technologies of identification couldn't play a useful (if limited) role in identifying potential terrorists, working in conjunction with the human intelligence that has proved to be the most effective way of catching and deterring serious criminals. But as the example of the Blob Machine shows, there is no reason to expect that technologies of identification will be designed in ways that target the guilty while sparing the innocent. There is a grave danger, in other words, that our emotional response to the new fears that menace us will lead us to adopt ineffective and unnecessarily invasive architectures of identification and risk profiling that could linger long after the fears that inspired them have passed.

In the pages that follow, I will argue that there is no need for this grim state of affairs to come to pass. It is possible to resist the excesses of the Naked Crowd—possible, that is, to design laws and technologies that protect liberty and security at the same time. But the challenge ahead will not be easy. Chapter 1, "A Cautionary Tale," takes us to Britain for a vision of a society in which the crowd's emotional demands for security are more or less unchecked by legal or constitutional restraints. In the face of widespread fears of terrorism, Britain wired itself up with thousands of surveillance cameras—a technology that (unlike the Blob Machine) threatens privacy and equality without empirically measurable benefits for security. Chapter 2, "The Psychology of Fear," explores the reasons why the crowd, left to its own devices, reacts to threats emotionally rather than analytically and is more concerned about feeling safe than being safe. As a result of these biases of public opinion, we are vulnerable to being terrorized by dramatic but low-probability events—acts of terror that inspire fear vastly disproportionate to the immediate human carnage left in their wake. Chapter 3, "The Silver Bullet," describes the search in Silicon Valley and Washington for security technologies that will protect individuals without requiring government officials to make discretionary human judgments about who is trustworthy and who is not. But although it is possible to design these technologies in ways that protect liberty as well as security, the technologists are more likely to choose designs that dramatically favor security over liberty: they are creatures of the market, and the market craves efficiency above all. Chapter 4, "The Path of the Law," argues that Congress is more likely than the courts to resist the public's demand for a zero-risk society. Legislators have proved to be more willing than judges to question the most sweeping claims of executive authority, although little more willing to demand that the most invasive searches and seizures are reserved for the most serious crimes. Chapter 5, "Identity Crisis," suggests that the crowd's unrealistic demand for a zero-risk society is related to our anxieties about identity. Because we can no longer rely on traditional markers of status to decide whom to trust, the crowd demands that individuals prove their trustworthiness by exposing as much personal information as possible; in an exhibitionistic and narcissistic age, individuals are happy to oblige in an effort to establish an emotional connection with the crowd.

In the epilogue, "An Escape from Fear," I explore ways that legislators, the courts, and the public itself might respond constructively to our modern anxieties in an effort to protect freedom, privacy, and security. In my view, political rather than judicial checks and balances provide the most promising avenues for regulation, although all of the relevant parties have a role to play. But the Naked Crowd wants what it wants, and tends to get what it demands, so it would be foolish to underestimate the challenges ahead.

At least the path we need to resist is clear. For a cautionary tale, please follow me to England.

CHAPTER ONE

A Cautionary Tale

A WEEK AFTER THE ATTACKS OF 9/11, AS MOST AMERI-
can stocks plummeted, a few companies, with products particularly well suited for a new and anxious age, soared in value.
One of the fastest-growing stocks was Visionics, whose price
more than tripled. The New Jersey company is an industry
leader in the fledgling science of biometrics, a method of identifying people by scanning and quantifying their unique physical characteristics—their facial structures, for example, or their
retinal patterns. Visionics manufactures a face-recognition
technology called FaceIt, which creates identification codes for
individuals based on eighty unique aspects of their facial structures, like the width of the nose and the location of the temples.
FaceIt can instantly compare an image of any individual's face
with a database of the faces of suspected terrorists, or anyone
else.

Visionics was quick to understand that the terrorist attacks
represented not only a tragedy but also a business opportunity.
On the afternoon of 9/11, the company sent out an e-mail mes-

sage to reporters, announcing that its founder and CEO, Joseph Atick, "has been speaking worldwide about the need for biometric systems to catch known terrorists and wanted criminals." On September 20, Atick testified before a special government committee appointed by the secretary of transportation. Atick's message—that security in airports and embassies could be improved using face-recognition technology as part of a comprehensive national surveillance plan that he called Operation Noble Shield—was greeted enthusiastically by members of the committee. To identify terrorists concealed in the crowd, Atick proposed to wire up Reagan National Airport in Washington and other vulnerable airports throughout the country with more than 300 cameras each. Cameras would scan the faces of passengers standing in line, and biometric technology would be used to analyze their faces and make sure they were not on an international terrorist watch list. More cameras unobtrusively installed throughout the airport could identify passengers as they walked through metal detectors and public areas. And a final scan could ensure that no suspected terrorist boarded a plane. "We have created a biometric network platform that turns every camera into a Web browser submitting images to a database in Washington, querying for matches," Atick said. "If a match occurs, it will set off an alarm in Washington, and someone will make a decision to wire the image to marshals at the airport."

Of course, protecting airports is only one aspect of homeland security: A terrorist could be lurking on any corner in America. In the wake of the 9/11 attacks, Howard Safir, the former New York police commissioner, recommended the installation of 100 biometric surveillance cameras in Times Square to scan the faces of pedestrians and compare them with a database of suspected terrorists. Atick told me that since the attacks, he has been approached by local and federal authorities from across the country about the possibility of installing biometric surveillance cameras in stadiums and subway systems and near national monuments. "The Office of Homeland Security might be the overall umbrella that will coordinate with local police forces" to install cameras linked to a biometric network throughout American cities, Atick suggested. "How can we be alerted when someone is entering the subway? How can we be sure when someone is entering Madison Square Garden? How can we protect monuments? We need to create an invisible fence, an invisible shield."

Before 9/11, the idea that Americans would voluntarily agree to live their lives under the gaze of a network of biometric surveillance cameras, peering at them in government buildings, shopping malls, subways, and stadiums, would have seemed unthinkable, a dystopian fantasy of a society that had surrendered privacy and anonymity. But after 9/11, the fear of terrorism was so overwhelming that people were happy to give up privacy without experiencing a corresponding increase in security. More concerned about feeling safe than actually being safe, they demanded the construction of vast technological architectures of surveillance even though the most reliable empirical studies suggested that the proliferation of surveillance cameras had "no effect on violent crime"[1] or terrorism. In this regard, however, America was at least a decade behind the times. In the 1990s, Britain experienced similar public demands for surveillance cameras as a feel-good response to fears of terrorism. And in Britain, the cameras were implemented on a wide scale, providing a cautionary tale about the dangers of constructing ineffective but popular architectures of surveillance that continue to expand after the initial fears that led to their installation have passed.

At the beginning of September 2001, I had gone to Britain to answer a question that seems far more pertinent today than it did when I arrived: Why would a free and flourishing Western democracy wire itself up with so many closed-circuit television cameras that it resembled the set of *Real World* or *The Truman Show*? The answer, I discovered, was fear of terrorism. In 1993 and 1994, two terrorist bombs planted by the IRA exploded in London's financial district, a historic and densely packed square mile known as the City of London. In response to widespread public anxiety about terrorism, the government decided to install a "ring of steel"—a network of closed-circuit television cameras mounted on the eight official entry gates that control access to the City. Anxiety about terrorism didn't go away, and the cameras in Britain continued to multiply. In 1994, a two-year-old boy named Jamie Bulger was kidnapped and murdered by two ten-year-old schoolboys, and surveillance cameras captured a grainy shot of the killers leading their victim out of a shopping center. Bulger's assailants couldn't, in fact, be identified on camera—they were caught because they boasted to their friends—but the video footage, replayed over and over again on television, shook the country to its core. Riding a wave of enthusiasm for closed-circuit television, or CCTV, created by the attacks, John Major's Conservative government decided to devote more than three-quarters of its crime-prevention budget to encourage local authorities to install CCTV. The promise of cameras as a magic bullet against crime and terrorism inspired one of Major's most successful campaign slogans: "If you've got nothing to hide, you've got nothing to fear."

Instead of being perceived as an Orwellian intrusion, the cameras in Britain proved to be extremely popular. They were hailed as the people's technology, a friendly eye in the sky, not Big Brother but a kindly and watchful uncle or aunt. Local governments couldn't get enough of them; each hamlet and fen in the British countryside wanted its own CCTV surveillance system, even when the most serious threat to public safety was coming from rampaging soccer fans. In 1994, 79 city centers had surveillance networks; by 1998, 440 city centers were wired, including all the major cities with a population over 500,000.[2] By the late 1990s, as part of its center-left campaign to be tough on crime, Tony Blair's New Labour government decided to support the cameras with a vengeance. Between 1996 and 1998, CCTV became the "single most heavily funded non-criminal justice crime prevention measure."[3] There are now so many cameras attached to so many different surveillance systems in the United Kingdom that people have stopped counting. According to one estimate, there are 4.2 million surveillance cameras in Britain,[4] and, in fact, there may be far more.

As I filed through customs at Heathrow Airport, there were cameras concealed in domes in the ceiling. There were cameras pointing at the ticket counters, at the escalators, and at the tracks as I waited for the Heathrow Express to Paddington Station. When I got out at Paddington, there were cameras on the platform and cameras on the pillars in the main terminal. Cameras followed me as I walked from the main station to the underground, and there were cameras at each of the stations on the way to King's Cross. Outside King's Cross, there were cameras trained on the bus stand and the taxi stand and the sidewalk, and still more cameras in the station. There were cameras on the backs of buses to record people who crossed into the wrong traffic lane. Throughout Britain today, there are speed cameras and red-light cameras, cameras in lobbies and elevators, in hotels and restaurants, in nursery schools and high schools. There are even cameras in hospitals. (After a raft of "baby thefts" in the early 1990s, the government gave hospitals money to install cameras in waiting rooms, maternity wards, and operating rooms.) And everywhere there are warning signs, announcing the presence of cameras with a jumble of different icons, slogans, and exhortations, from the bland "CCTV in Operation" to the peppy "CCTV: Watching for You!" By one estimate, the average Briton is now photographed by more than 300 separate cameras from 30 separate CCTV networks in a single day.[5]

BRITAIN'S EXPERIENCE UNDER the watchful eye of the CCTV cameras is a vision of what Americans can expect if we choose to go down the same road in our efforts to achieve homeland security. Although the cameras in Britain were initially justified as a way of combating terrorism, they soon came to serve very different functions: Seven hundred cameras now record the license plate number of every car that enters central London during peak hours, to confirm that the drivers have paid a £5 traffic-abatement tax. (Those who haven't paid are charged a fine.)[6] The cameras are designed not to produce arrests but to make people feel that they are being watched at all times. Instead of keeping terrorists off planes, biometric surveillance is being used to keep punks out of shopping malls. The people behind the live video screens are zooming in on unconventional behavior in public that, in fact, has nothing to do with terrorism. And rather than thwarting serious crime, the cameras are being used for different purposes that Americans may prefer to avoid.

The dream of a biometric surveillance system that can identify people's faces in public places and separate the innocent from the guilty is not new. Clive Norris, a criminologist at the University of Hull, is Britain's leading authority on the social effects of CCTV. In his definitive study, *The Maximum Surveillance Society: The Rise of CCTV,* Norris notes that in the nineteenth century, police forces in England and France began to focus on how to distinguish the casual offender from the "habitual criminal" who might evade detection by moving from town to town. In the 1870s, Alphonse Bertillon, a records clerk at the prefecture of police in Paris, used his knowledge of statistics and anthropomorphic measurements to create a system for comparing the thousands of photographs of arrested suspects in Parisian police stations. He took a series of measurements—of skull size, for example, and the distance between the ear and chin—and created a unique code for every suspect whom the police had photographed. Photographs were then grouped according to the codes, and a new suspect could be compared only with the photos that had similar measurements, instead of with the entire portfolio. A procedure that had taken hours or days was now reduced to a few minutes. Although widely adopted, Bertillon's system was hard for unskilled clerks to administer. For this reason, it was edged out, as an identification system, by the fingerprint, championed by Francis Galton, the founder of the eugenics movement, who saw fingerprints as a way of classifying "hereditary" criminals.[7]

It wasn't until the 1980s, with the development of computerized biometric and other face-recognition systems, that Bertillon's dream became feasible on a broad scale. In the course of studying how biometric scanning could be used to authenticate the identities of people who sought admission to secure buildings, innovators like Joseph Atick realized that the same technology could be used to pick suspects or license plates out of a crowd. It's the license plate technology that the London police have found most attractive, because it tends to be more reliable: In 1996, the City of London adopted a predecessor to the current automated license-plate-recognition system that records the plates of all cars entering and leaving the city. The stored license plate numbers are compared with a database of those of stolen cars, and the system can set off alarms whenever a suspicious car enters the city.[8] By contrast with this relatively effective license-plate-recognition system, a test of the best face-recognition systems, funded by the U.S. Department of Defense, found that they failed to identify matches a third of the time.[9] And a review by the International Biometrics Group, an impartial industry trade organization, found that facial-scan technologies have very high false rejection rates over time, and that they have trouble identifying people with darker skin, as well as people who change their hairstyles or facial hair.

Soon after arriving in London, I visited the CCTV monitoring room in the City of London police station, where the British war against terrorism began. On the corner of Love Lane, the station has two cameras pointed at the entrance and a sign by the door inviting citizens to "Rat on a Rat: Call Crime Stoppers Anonymously." I was met by the press officer, Tim Parsons, and led up to the control station, a modest-size installation that looks like an air-traffic-control room, with uniformed officers scanning two rows of monitors in search of car thieves and traffic offenders. "The technology here is geared up to terrorism," Parsons told me. "The fact that we're getting ordinary people—burglars stealing cars—as a result of it is sort of a bonus." "Have you caught any terrorists?" I asked. "No, not using this technology, no," he replied.

As we watched the monitors, rows of slow-moving cars filed through the gates into the City, and cameras recorded their license plate numbers and the faces of the drivers. After several minutes, one monitor set off a soft, pinging alarm. We had a match! But, no, it was a false alarm. The license plate that set off the system was 8620bmc, but the number of the stolen car recorded in the database was 8670amc. After a few more mismatches, the machine finally found an offender, though not a serious one. A red van had gone through a speed camera, and the local authority that issued the ticket couldn't identify the driver. An alert went out on the central police national computer, and it set off the alarm when the van entered the City. "We're not going to do anything about it because it's not a desperately important call," said the sergeant on duty.

Because the cameras on the "ring of steel" surrounding the City take clear pictures of each driver's face, I asked whether the City used the biometric facial-recognition technology that American airports are now being urged to adopt. "We're experimenting with it to see if we could pick faces out of the crowd, but the technology is not sufficiently good enough,"

Parsons said. "The system that I saw demonstrated two or three years ago, a lot of the time it couldn't differentiate between a man and a woman." Nevertheless, Parsons insisted that the technology will become more accurate. "It's just a matter of time. Then we can use it to detect the presence of criminals on foot in the city," he said.

In the future, as face-recognition technology becomes more accurate, it will become even more intrusive, because of pressures to expand the biometric database. I mentioned to Joseph Atick of Visionics that the City of London was thinking about using his technology to establish a database that would include not only terrorists but also all British citizens whose faces were registered with the national driver's license bureau. If that occurs, every citizen who walks the streets of the City could be instantly identified by the police and evaluated in light of his or her past misdeeds, no matter how trivial. With the impatience of a rationalist, Atick dismissed the possibility. "Technically, they won't be able to do it without coming back to me," he said. "They will have to justify it to me." Atick struck me as a refined and thoughtful man (he is the former director of the Computational Neuroscience Laboratory at Rockefeller University), but it seems odd to put the liberties of a democracy in the hands of one unelected scientist, no matter how well supervised he may be.

Atick says that his technology is an enlightened alternative to racial and ethnic profiling, and if the faces in the biometric database were, in fact, restricted to known terrorists, his argument might be convincing. Instead of stopping all passengers who appear to be Middle Eastern and victimizing thousands of innocent people, the system could focus with laserlike precision on a handful of the guilty. (This assumes that the terrorists aren't cunning enough to disguise themselves.) But when I asked whether any of the existing biometric databases in England or America are limited to suspected terrorists, Atick confessed that they aren't. There is a simple reason for this: Few terrorists are suspected in advance of their crimes. For this reason, cities in England and elsewhere have tried to justify their investment in face-recognition systems by filling their databases with those troublemakers whom the authorities can easily identify: local criminals. When FaceIt technology was used to scan the faces of the thousands of fans entering the Super Bowl in Tampa, for example, the matches produced by the database weren't terrorists. They were low-level ticket scalpers and pickpockets.

Biometrics is a feel-good technology that is being marketed based on a false promise—that the database will be limited to suspected terrorists. But the FaceIt technology, as it's now being used in England, isn't really intended to catch terrorists at all. It's intended to scare local hoodlums into thinking they might be setting off alarms even when the cameras are turned off. I came to understand this "Wizard of Oz" aspect of the technology when I visited Bob Lack's monitoring station in the London borough of Newham. A former London police officer, Lack attracted national attention—including a visit from Tony Blair—by pioneering the use of face-recognition technology before other people were convinced that it was entirely reliable. What Lack grasped early on was that reliability was in many ways beside the point.

Lack installed his first CCTV system in 1997, and he intentionally exaggerated its powers from the beginning. "We put one camera out and twelve signs" announcing the presence of cameras, Lack told me. "We reduced crime by sixty percent in the area where we posted the signs. Then word on the street went out that we had dummy cameras." So Lack turned his attention to face-recognition technology and tried to create the impression that far more people's faces were in the database than actually were. "We've designed a poster now about making Newham a safe place for a family," he said. "And we're telling the criminal we have this information on him: We know his name; we know his address; we know what crimes he commits." It's not true, Lack admitted, "but then, we're entitled to disinform some people, aren't we?" "So you're telling the criminal that you know his name even though you don't," I asked. "Right," Lack replied. "Pretty much that's about advertising, isn't it?"

Lack was elusive when I asked him who, exactly, was in his database. "I don't know," he replied, noting that the local police chief decided who went into the database. He would only make an "educated guess" that the database contained 100 "violent street robbers" under the age of eighteen. "You have to have been convicted of a crime—nobody suspected goes on, unless they're a suspected murderer—and there has to be sufficient police intelligence to say you are committing those crimes and have been so in the last twelve weeks." When I asked for the written standards that determined who, precisely, was put in the database, and what crimes they had to have committed, Lack never produced them.

From Lack's point of view, it didn't matter who was in his database, because his system wasn't designed to catch terrorists or violent criminals. In the three years that the system had been up and running, it hadn't resulted in a single arrest. "I'm not in the business of having people arrested," Lack said. "The deterrent value has far exceeded anything you imagine." The alarms went off an average of three times a day during the month of August 2001, but the only people Lack would conclusively identify were local youths who had volunteered to be put in the database as part of an "intensive surveillance supervision program," as an alternative to serving a custodial sentence. "The public statements about the efficacy of the Newham facial-recognition system bear little relationship to its actual operational capabilities, which are rather weak and poor," I was told by Clive Norris of the University of Hull. "They want everyone to believe that they are potentially under scrutiny. Its effectiveness, perhaps, is based on a lie."

This lie has a venerable place in the philosophy of surveillance. In his preface to *Panopticon,* Jeremy Bentham imagined the social benefits of a ring-shaped "inspection-house" whose inmates could be subject to constant surveillance by monitors in a central inspection tower who were concealed by venetian blinds. Uncertain about whether or not they were being watched, the inhabitants would be inhibited from engaging in antisocial behavior. Michel Foucault described the purpose of the Panopticon—"to induce in the inmate a state of conscious and permanent visibility that assures the automatic functioning of power."[10] Foucault predicted that this condition of ubiquitous, unverifiable surveillance would come to define the modern age.

Britain, at the moment, is not quite the Panopticon, because its various camera networks aren't linked and there aren't enough operators to watch all the cameras. But over the next few years, that seems likely to change, as Britain moves toward an integrated Web-based surveillance system. Today, for example, the surveillance systems for the London underground and the British police feed into separate control rooms, but Sergio Velastin, a computer-vision scientist, says he believes the two systems will eventually be linked, using digital technology. Velastin is working on behavioral-recognition technology for the London and Paris subway systems that can look for unusual movements in crowds, setting off an alarm, for example, when people appear to be fighting or trying to jump on the tracks. (Because human CCTV operators are easily bored and distracted, automatic alarms are viewed as the wave of the future.) After ten years of research, Velastin and his colleagues have produced a system called the Modular Intelligent Pedestrian Surveillance Architecture, which can be programmed to detect unusual situations—such as stationary loiterers or unaccompanied bags—and to alert the operator with automated alarms.[11] "Imagine you see a piece of unattended baggage which might contain a bomb," Velastin told me. "You can back-drag on the image and locate the person who left it there. You can say, 'Where did that person come from and where is that person now?' You can conceive in the future that you might be able to do that for every person in every place in the system." Without social agreement and legal restrictions on how the system could be deployed, it could create a kind of ubiquitous surveillance that the government could use to harass its political enemies or that citizens could use, with the help of subpoenas, to blackmail or embarrass one another.

Once thousands of cameras from hundreds of separate CCTV systems are able to feed their digital images to a central monitoring station, and the images can be analyzed with face- and behavioral-recognition software to identify unusual patterns, then the possibilities of the Panopticon will suddenly become very real. And few people doubt that connectivity is around the corner. Stephen Graham has predicted gloomily that CCTV will become the fifth utility, following the pattern of gas, electricity, water, and telecommunications, which began as disconnected networks in the nineteenth century and were eventually standardized, integrated, and ubiquitous.[12]

At the moment, there is only one fully integrated CCTV system in Britain: It transmits digital images over a broadband wireless network, like the one Joseph Atick has proposed for American airports, rather than relying on traditional video cameras that are chained to dedicated cables. It is located in the fading city of Hull, Britain's leading timber port, about three hours northeast of London. Hull has traditionally been associated not with dystopian fantasies but with fantasies of a more basic sort: For hundreds of years, it has been the prostitution capital of northeastern Britain. Six years ago, a heroin epidemic created an influx of addicted young women who took to streetwalking to sustain their drug habits. Nearly two years ago, the residents association of a low-income housing project called the Goodwin Centre hired a likable and enterprising young civil engineer named John Marshall to address the problem of underage prostitutes having sex on people's windowsills. When Marshall met me at the Hull railway station, he identified himself by carrying a CCTV warning sign. Armed with more than $1 million in public financing from the European Union, Marshall decided to build what he calls the world's first Ethernet-based, wireless CCTV system.

Initially, Marshall put up twenty-seven cameras around the housing project. The cameras didn't bother the prostitutes, who in fact felt safer working under CCTV. Instead, they scared the johns—especially after the police recorded their license numbers, banged on their doors, and threatened to publish their names in the newspapers. Business plummeted, and the prostitutes moved indoors or across town to the traditional red-light district, where the city decided to tolerate their presence in limited numbers. But Marshall soon realized that he had bigger fish to fry than displacing prostitutes from one part of Hull to another. His innovative network of linked cameras attracted national attention, which led to $20 million in grant money from various levels of government to expand the surveillance network throughout the city of Hull. "In a year and a half," Marshall says, "there'll be a digital connection to every household in the city. As far as cameras go, I can imagine that, in ten years' time, the whole city will be covered. That's the speed that CCTV is growing." In the world that Marshall imagines, every household in Hull will be linked to a central network that can access cameras trained inside and outside every building in the city.

The person who controls access to this network of intimate images will be a very powerful person indeed. And so I was eager to meet the monitors of the Panopticon for myself. On a side street of Hull, near the Star and Garter Pub and the city morgue, the Goodwin Centre's monitoring station is housed inside a ramshackle private-security firm called Sentry Alarms Ltd. The sign over the door reads "The Guard House." The monitoring station is locked behind a thick, black, vault-style door, but it looks like a college computer center, with an Alicia

Silverstone pinup near the outrance. Instead of an impressive video wall, there are only two small desktop computers, which receive all the signals from the Goodwin Centre network. And the digital, Web-based images—unlike traditional video—are surprisingly fuzzy and jerky, like streaming video transmitted over a slow modem.

During my time in the control room, from 9 P.M. to midnight, I experienced firsthand a phenomenon that critics of CCTV surveillance have often described: When you put a group of bored, unsupervised men in front of live video screens and allow them to zoom in on whatever happens to catch their eye, they tend to spend a fair amount of time leering at women. "What catches the eye is groups of young men and attractive young women," I was told by Clive Norris, the Hull criminologist. "It's what we call a sense of the obvious." There are plenty of stories of video voyeurism: A control room in the Midlands, for example, took close-up shots of women with large breasts and taped them up on the walls. In Hull, this temptation is magnified by the fact that part of the operators' job is to keep an eye on prostitutes. As it got late, though, there weren't enough prostitutes to keep us entertained, so we kept ourselves awake by scanning the streets in search of the purely consensual activities of boyfriends and girlfriends making out in cars. "She had her legs wrapped around his waist a minute ago," one of the operators said appreciatively as we watched two teenagers go at it.

Norris also found that operators, in addition to focusing on attractive young women, tend to focus on young men, especially those with dark skin. "Over a third of the people were looked at merely on the basis of belonging to a particular category—for

being young or black or scruffy—not on the basis of their behavior or their behavioral characteristic," Norris says. And
those young men know they are being watched: CCTV is far
less popular among black men than among British men as a
whole. In Hull and elsewhere, rather than eliminating prejudi-
cial surveillance and racial profiling, CCTV surveillance has
tended to amplify it.

After returning from the digital city of Hull, I had a clearer
understanding of how, precisely, the spread of CCTV cameras
is transforming British society and why I think it's important
for America to resist going down the same path. "I actually
don't think the cameras have had much effect on crime rates,"
says Jason Ditton, a criminologist at the University of Sheffield,
whose evaluation of the effect of the cameras in Glasgow found
no clear reduction in violent crime. "We've had a fall in crime
in the last ten years, and CCTV proponents say it's because of
the cameras. I'd say it's because we had a boom economy in the
last seven years and a fall in unemployment." In 2000, Britain's
violent-crime rates actually increased by 4.3 percent, even
though the cameras continued to proliferate.[13] But CCTV cameras have a mysterious knack for justifying themselves regardless of what happens to crime. When crime goes up, the
cameras get the credit for detecting it, and when crime goes
down, they get the credit for preventing it. "It's not subject to
normal canons of proof because belief in it is religious," says
Ditton. "When you question its powers, the British get upset,
as if you're questioning the existence of God."

In 2002, the British Home Office conducted a comprehensive review of the twenty-two most reliable empirical studies in
the United Kingdom and the United States about the relation-

ship between CCTV and crime reduction. The review concluded that "CCTV is most effective in reducing vehicle crime in car parks, but it had little or no effect on crime in public transport and city centre settings."[14] In particular, the review noted that "CCTV had no effect on violent crimes" (from five studies) and that the only category of crimes where it had a "significant desirable effect" (from eight studies) was in reducing vehicle thefts in parking lots.[15] But even here, the survey cautioned that the success of CCTV schemes in parking lots was accompanied by other factors such as improved lighting, painting, fencing, payment schemes, and security personnel. When it came to crime committed outside of parking lots, however, the connection between the cameras and crime reduction was hard to discern. In city center areas, "there was evidence that CCTV led to a negligible reduction in crime of about two percent in experimental areas" in five U.K. settings "but had no effect on crime in the four North American evaluations."[16] And in public transport systems, the evidence was both mixed and unimpressive: One study found no effect on crime, one found that crime increased after the cameras were installed, and two studies found that crime declined slightly, but that it wasn't clear that the slight decline was due to the cameras or to other factors.[17]

If the creation of a surveillance society in Britain hasn't prevented terrorist attacks, or reduced violent or nonviolent crime in a meaningful way, it has had subtle but far-reaching social costs. The handful of privacy advocates in Britain have tried to enumerate those costs by arguing that the cameras invade privacy, changing the character of social space in the process. For example, Simon Davies of Privacy International notes that people who are always unsure about whether they are being watched feel a powerful urge to prove their innocence. "I bought a newspaper recently and realized I hadn't got a receipt," Davies recalls. "I realized I could be accused of stealing the paper, but then a little voice in my brain said, 'Don't worry, it will be on film.' This is the most dangerous side of the technology, because now it becomes the people's technology. It's for us to prove that we're good and honest." Other people behave in similarly self-conscious ways under the cameras, bristling at the imputation of guilt that comes from being watched. Inside a monitoring room in Guilford, I saw a group of teenagers who noticed that a camera was pivoting around to follow them; they gave it the finger and looked back over their shoulders as they tried to escape its gaze.

The cameras are also a powerful inducement toward social conformity for citizens who can't be sure whether they are being watched. "I am gay and I might want to kiss my boyfriend in Victoria Square at two in the morning," a supporter of the cameras in Hull told me. "I would not kiss my boyfriend now. I am aware that it has altered the way I might behave. . . . Something like that might be regarded as an offense against public decency. This isn't San Francisco." Nevertheless, the man insisted that the benefits of the cameras outweighed the costs, because "thousands of people feel safer."

In addition to threatening privacy and promoting social conformity, the cameras are in tension with values of equality. They are ways of putting people in their place, of deciding who gets in and who stays out, of limiting people's movement and restricting their opportunities. I came to appreciate the exclusionary potential of the surveillance technology in a relatively low-tech way when I visited a shopping center in Uxbridge, a suburb of London. The manager of the center explained that people who are observed to be misbehaving in the mall can be banned from the premises. The banning process isn't very complicated. "Because this isn't public property, we have the right to refuse entry, and if there's a wrongdoer, we give them a note or a letter, or simply tell them, 'You're banned.'" In America, this would provoke anyone who was banned to call Alan Dershowitz and sue for discrimination. But the British are less litigious and more willing to defer to authority. "We banned two little boys who were wearing white masks and frightening customers," the manager recalled. "One of the mums called me up. She said, 'Look, John, I trust you. You're a fair man. Do you think that's really my little boy?' She had no idea." The manager looked at the CCTV tapes and assured her that "the little horror was indeed her Jimmy." She accepted his verdict without complaint.

Banning people from shopping malls is only the beginning. A couple of days before I was in London, Borders Books announced the installation of a biometric face-recognition surveillance system in its flagship store on Charing Cross Road. Borders' scheme meant that anyone who had shoplifted in the past was permanently branded as a shoplifter in the future. In response to howls of protest from corporate headquarters in America, Borders dismantled the system, but it may well be resurrected in a post-9/11 age. As David Lyon has argued, a world in which people are followed throughout life by their past misdeeds is one in which we can no longer be a customer in one context and a convicted shoplifter in another: The "data image" of shoplifter has the potential to become a master status that serves as an engine of exclusion.[18]

Perhaps one reason that Britain has embraced the new technologies of surveillance, while America, at least before 9/11, has strenuously resisted them, is that British society is more accepting of social classifications than we are. The British desire to put people in their place is a central focus of British literature, from Dickens to John Osborne and Alan Bennett. The work of George Orwell that casts the most light on Britain's swooning embrace of CCTV is not *Nineteen Eighty-Four*. It is Orwell's earlier book *The English People*. "Exaggerated class distinctions have been diminishing," Orwell wrote, but "the great majority of the people can still be 'placed' in an instant by their manners, clothes and general appearance"[19] and, above all, their accents. Class distinctions are less hardened today than they were when I was a student at Oxford at the height of the Thatcher-era *Brideshead Revisited* chic. But it's no surprise that a society long accustomed to the idea that people should know their place didn't hesitate to embrace a technology designed to ensure that people stay in their assigned places. In *Privacy and Freedom,* Alan Westin traced America's and Britain's different attitudes toward privacy to their different forms of democracy. Britain, he wrote, has a "deferential democratic balance" characterized by a strong trust in authority, "a relatively homogeneous population, strong family structure, surviving class system, positive public attitude toward government, and elite systems of education and government service." This produces a culture with great personal reserve and "faith in government that bestows major areas of privacy for government operations."[20] By contrast, the United States has an "egalitarian democratic balance," characterized by greater individualism. This produces more suspicion of government secrecy and less tolerance for state invasions of individual privacy. It's true that Britain and America share a certain resistance to being bossed about by centralized government, but this suspicion expresses itself in different ways. The British are anarchic communitarians, more moved by arguments about fair play than legalistic protections. Almost in the same breath, they have repealed century-old legal protections for habeas corpus and constructed royal commissions of inquiry that, in the end, freed suspects wrongly accused of terrorism in Northern Ireland. The more legalistic and individualistic Americans, by contrast, resist encroachments on their formal rights and display a more instinctive distrust of government authority in all its forms. Most important of all, America, unlike Britain, has a constitutional separation of powers; after 9/11 this enabled Congress to check the incessant demands by the executive and the public to expand surveillance authority in all its forms.

Will America be able to resist the pressure to follow the British example and wire itself up with surveillance cameras and biometric identification systems? Before 9/11, it seemed clear that we would. Like Germany and France, which are squeamish about CCTV because of their experience with twentieth-century totalitarianism, Americans have been less willing than the British to trust the government and defer to authority. Indeed, months before his apotheosis as the hero of the NAS-DAQ, Joseph Atick of Visionics had been under siege by privacy advocates, from House Majority Leader Dick Armey to the ACLU, for deploying his face-recognition technology at the

Tampa Super Bowl. In America, unlike Britain, a strong civil liberties tradition uniting conservative libertarians on the right with civil libertarians on the left had, over the course of the 1990s, kept the cameras from being widely deployed: By 1997, hardly more than sixty urban centers in America had installed any kind of CCTV system at all.[21]

After 9/11, we were told repeatedly that everything had changed. In the weeks after the attacks, an ABC/*Washington Post* poll found that 66 percent of those surveyed were willing to give up some of their civil liberties to prevent further terrorist activities.[22] And in the months after the attack, the camera peddlers had more success than they had known before. Visionics announced that its FaceIt system was being tested at the Dallas/Fort Worth and Palm Beach International Airports, as well as Logan International Airport; and, in a small if perverse coup, FaceIt cameras were installed to scan visitors to the Statue of Liberty. But Joseph Atick's dreams of building a Noble Shield at every airport in the land failed to materialize in light of evidence about the technology's relatively low accuracy, and Visionics' stock soon fell from its post-9/11 highs.

Even more telling was the response to a report that the Metropolitan Police Department in Washington, D.C., had activated a high-tech command center that it envisioned as the centerpiece of the most far-reaching surveillance network in the nation. The Washington police used video surveillance for the first time in April 2000, when they installed cameras to monitor street protests at the World Bank and the International Monetary Fund. The experiment was considered such a success that the department proceeded to build a $7 million control room to coordinate more extensive surveillance. The control room was used for the first time on 9/11, when officials from the Secret Service, FBI, and Capitol Police joined forces with local police officers in monitoring activities at buildings around the capital. But it escaped public notice until February 2002, when *The Wall Street Journal* reported that the police intended to expand its operations.

"In the context of September 11, we have no choice but to accept greater use of this technology," said Stephen Gaffigan, the head of the project, adding that he was "intrigued" by the British model of surveillance.[23] The control room now receives feeds from more than 12 cameras in downtown Washington, focused on the White House, the National Mall, and Union Station, and from others mounted on police helicopters. It was designed to accept signals from 200 more cameras in the Washington Metro and another 200 in Washington public schools that were installed after two teenagers shot their classmates at Columbine High School in Littleton, Colorado. Eventually, the Washington police said they planned to accept video feeds from private businesses, including shopping malls and apartment buildings, which could then be beamed from the command center to mobile units in more than 1,000 police cars throughout the city. Because the system is fully digital, wireless, and encrypted, it could be monitored from a federal command center buried in the Rocky Mountains in the event of a nuclear attack, or from Salt Lake City during the Olympics. Eventually, the surveillance network will be able to link and monitor subway stations, schools, and city streets.[24]

Soon after its existence became public, I visited the Washington command center, in Room 5056 of police headquarters. It had a high-tech sheen that made the 1980s-era control rooms in Britain look like fading sets from an *Austin Powers* movie. There were wall-to-ceiling plasma screens and forty video monitors. There was a safe room behind the screens built to the CIA's security specifications. There was a leather chair for the commander in charge of operations. A yellow alert symbol announced that there was "a significant risk of terrorist attacks"—the first high alert since 9/11. A huge banner reproduced George W. Bush's Churchillian motto for the war on terrorism: "We will not tire, we will not falter, we will not fail." The lieutenant in charge zoomed in on two young African American teenagers who were loitering by Union Station. The digital picture was far clearer than its British counterparts, but the lieutenant in charge said he could make the image even clearer after cleaning it up on the computer. He clicked the mouse and a three-dimensional geospatial map of the area around the World Bank Building appeared. "This is what we used during the last demonstration," he said. "It's very accurate down to shrubs and manhole covers. It can simulate crowds and simulate a group of demonstrators trying to run through a police perimeter and destroy property. It allows us to record where everyone is during the course of a live event."

Before 9/11, the Washington surveillance system had been activated only for limited periods during events that seemed to pose special threats, such as the World Bank meeting and the presidential inauguration. But Gaffigan told me that the police department had been approached by neighborhood associations throughout Washington and would be pleased to wire up various neighborhoods in response to popular demand, using the cameras for general deterrence of street crime, rather than crowd control during public emergencies. "The next logical extension is into communities to aid our crime-fighting efforts," Gaffigan told *The Wall Street Journal*, noting that shopkeepers in Georgetown had already proposed linking their cameras to the central command center at their own expense. "People in England have easily adapted to it," Gaffigan said. "There has not been an outcry about privacy there."[25]

After visiting the center, I saw no reason to doubt that surveillance cameras in America could expand along the same lines as surveillance cameras in England. Originally justified as a way of protecting the capital city against terrorism, the cameras seemed poised to morph, in the face of popular demand, into a general but ineffective system of surveillance focused on low-level street crime. And yet, as it turned out, the political debate about the cameras evolved rather differently in England and America. Despite the support of community leaders in Washington, who demanded more cameras as a way of making their constituents feel safer, the vigorous coalition of libertarian conservatives and civil libertarian liberals that had opposed the cameras before 9/11 converged again to oppose their expansion. After several hearings before the city council, where the case against the cameras was forcefully presented, the Metropolitan Police Department retreated from its original plans. It abandoned an early draft of its proposed regulations, which had promised to use the cameras "to deter and/or eliminate crime in residential and commercial areas." In the face of libertarian opposition, the department promised to use the cameras only in exigent circumstances and not for "general crime deterrence," unless legislation was enacted to the contrary. The regulations also pledged that the cameras would be turned on only for limited time periods, at the direction of the chief of police, and that recorded images would ordinarily be erased after ten days. The city council endorsed the regulations, but it also unwisely funded a so-called pilot program to allow cameras to be put up in Washington neighborhoods and to study their effect on general crime prevention, detection, deterrence, and investigation. The council was unmoved by the fact that all of the most reliable empirical studies have found no convincing connection between the spread of the cameras and the decline of crime. And with far more sophisticated technology, an American system of linked cameras could become an even more powerful tool for political harassment.

As I write, America is at a crossroads, and it is difficult to say what the future of video surveillance will bring. In a survey of 190 people called for jury duty in Florida in 2002, the legal scholar Christopher Slobogin found that the respondents considered overt monitoring by street cameras where the tapes were not destroyed to be highly invasive, only slightly less so than a police search of a bedroom or a body cavity search at a border. By contrast, the respondents viewed monitoring cameras at national monuments, airports, and train stations without stored tapes to be minimally invasive, only slightly more so than the health and safety inspection of a factory.[26] This suggests that Americans may be sensitive to the difference between real time and archived forms of surveillance, and could be moved to object if poorly designed and highly invasive systems proliferate without regulation. As Slobogin's jurors recognized, there are certainly high-security events, such as presidential inaugurations and World Bank meetings, when general video surveillance of particular areas might be justified, as long as it's limited in duration and scope. But if the American system follows the path of the English system, it would be foolish to expect the courts to save us. As we will see in chapter 4, American constitutional law, in its current form, is unprepared to regulate a network of ubiquitous surveillance, in which the combination of linked camera systems and digital archives of tapes could make possible, in the not-so-distant future, dragnet surveillance of any individual who strikes the fancy of an unseen official at any time or any place in the country. Instead, Congress has proved more effective than the courts in checking the excesses of the president and public.

Of course, there are some liberties that should be sacrificed in times of national emergency if these sacrifices give us greater security. But Britain's experience in the fight against terrorism suggests that people may give up liberties without experiencing a corresponding increase in security. And if we meekly accede in the construction of vast feel-good architectures of surveillance that have far-reaching social costs and few discernible social benefits, we may find, in calmer times, that they are impossible to dismantle.

It's important to be precise about the choice we are facing. No one is threatening at the moment to turn America into Orwell's Big Brother. And Britain hasn't yet been turned into Big Brother, either. Many of the CCTV monitors and camera operators and policemen and entrepreneurs who took the time to meet with me were models of the British sense of fair play and respect for the rules. In many ways, the closed-circuit television cameras have only exaggerated the qualities of the British national character that Orwell identified in his less famous book: the acceptance of social hierarchy combined with the gentleness that leads people to wait in orderly lines at taxi stands; a deference to authority combined with an appealing tolerance of hypocrisy. These English qualities have their charms, but they are not American qualities. The promise of America is a promise that we can escape from the Old World, a world where people know their place.

When we say we are fighting for an open society, we don't mean a transparent society—one where neighbors can peer into one another's windows using the joysticks on their laptops. We mean a society open to the possibility that people can redefine and reinvent themselves every day; a society in which people can travel from place to place without showing their papers and being encumbered by their past; a society that respects privacy and constantly reshuffles social hierarchy. One ideal of America insists that your opportunities shouldn't be limited by your profile in a database, that no doors should be permanently closed to anyone who has the wrong smart card. If the twenty-first century proves to be a time when this ideal is abandoned—a time of surveillance cameras and creepy biometric face-scanning in Times Square—then Osama bin Laden will have inflicted an even more terrible blow than we now imagine.

CHAPTER TWO

The Psychology of Fear

IN 1987, TWO SCRAP-METAL DEALERS TROLLING FOR junk in an abandoned clinic in Goiânia, Brazil, came upon a discarded radiation machine that had been used for cancer therapy. Uncertain about what it was, they hoped that it might have some scrap value; and so they took the machine home and tried to saw it open. What resulted was one of the most serious radiation accidents in history. The source capsule ruptured, releasing radioactive cesium chloride salt, which glowed blue like carnival glitter. The dealers sold the remnants of the toxic machine for scrap to a junkyard owner; fascinated by the glowing blue glitter, the owner, in turn, distributed it to delighted friends and relatives. Over the next five days, these unlucky recipients began to develop gastrointestinal pain as a result of their exposure to radiation. By the time someone took the remains of the source capsule to the public health department, 249 people had been contaminated with radiation poisoning; scores were hospitalized and four eventually died.[1]

Initially, there was little coverage of the accident. But after a sensational account appeared on television, a nationwide panic ensued. Television reporters descended on the region and reports of "deadly glitter" and "glittering poison" soon were broadcast around the world. In the first weeks after the media coverage began, more than 100,000 residents lined up for radiation monitoring, and the wholesale value of agricultural products in the region fell by 50 percent, even though there was no evidence that any products had been contaminated. Housing prices near the accident scene plummeted; hotels lost thousands of reservations and tourism dried up.[2] Even more dramatically, residents of Goiânia became objects of fear and loathing throughout Brazil. They were turned away by the busload from hotels and airplanes; later, cars with license plates from Goiânia were stoned.[3] Goiânia was so dramatically branded in the public mind with the stigma of contamination that its public image was literally transformed: After the disaster, the international radiation sign was added to the Goiás state flag. The accident had changed the way the residents of Goiânia were perceived by their fellow citizens, and they marked the change by altering the symbol of their identity.

The accident in Goiânia resulted in only a handful of deaths, but it is a vivid example of how the public responds emotionally to widely publicized and highly terrifying events. And it shows how vulnerable America would be to something like a dirty bomb, whose radioactive core is the same cesium 137 that terrified the citizens of Brazil. A dirty bomb, like the radiation accident in Goiânia, would kill relatively few people at first—only the handful who were in its immediate vicinity—and, over the long term, would increase cancer rates in far fewer people than the number who died in the World Trade Center.

But the terror produced by a dirty bomb that was detonated in downtown Washington, D.C., for example, would make the Goiânia accident look tame: Amplified by 24/7 cable TV channels and broadcast repeatedly to a transfixed nation, the pictures of the contaminated scene would create panic entirely disproportionate to the radioactive threat, perhaps requiring the evacuation of large portions of the capital city and billions of dollars in cleanup. The government might be brought to a halt, and the constitutional structures that maintained a fragile equilibrium after 9/11 might be tested beyond the breaking point.

In this chapter, I'd like to examine why public fear leads people to react to remote but terrifying risks in emotional rather than analytical terms. Dramatic pictures of an accident with relatively few fatalities can create ripples of fear that stigmatize places, technologies, and even people long after the immediate danger has passed. This public fear is the most important barrier to efforts to design laws and technologies that protect liberty and security at the same time, and it has led the public to embrace technologies that threaten liberty without increasing security. But when the public is addressed in terms that it can trust and understand, it may react more calmly in the face of unfamiliar risks whose probability is hard to measure.

Paul Slovic of the University of Oregon is the nation's leading authority on the perception of risk. His work suggests that because the public thinks in terms of images rather than arguments, it has a hard time evaluating levels of risk after a person or place has been stigmatized in a highly visible way. Slovic draws on the work of the great sociologist Erving Goffman, whose study of stigma and social identity began by noting that "the Greeks, who were apparently strong on visual aids, originated the term stigma to refer to bodily signs designed to expose something unusual and bad about the moral status of the signifier. The signs were cut or burnt into the body and advertised that the bearer was a slave, a criminal, or a traitor—a blemished person, ritually polluted, to be avoided, especially in public places."[4]

Goffman was especially interested in the ways that a stranger can be discredited before the crowd by possessing a visible attribute that causes him or her to be "reduced in our minds from a whole and usual person to a tainted, discounted one." This attribute is a stigma, and Goffman said that it led to a "discrepancy between virtual and actual social identity."[5] Writing in the early 1960s, Goffman distinguished between three types of stigma that could lead an individual to be shunned or discriminated against—physical deformities and other "abominations of the body"; blemishes of individual character such as "weak will, domineering or unnatural passions, treacherous and rigid beliefs, and dishonesty, these being inferred from a known record of, for example, mental disorder, imprisonment, addiction, alcoholism, homosexuality, unemployment, suicidal attempts, and radical political behavior"; and finally, "the tribal stigma of race, nation and religion."[6]

As Goffman's list of "unnatural passions" and tribal stigmas makes clear, Americans in the postwar era were publicly stigmatized when they failed to conform to the conventional social expectations about morality and identity. Today, by contrast, those who fail to express public respect for another individual's personal choices about his or her identity—revealing themselves to be judgmental, arrogant, hierarchical, elitist, racist, or sexist—can experience public shame and ignominy as cutting as anything the Victorians could inflict. Sometimes, this shame can be alleviated only by publicly confessing to the shortcomings of character that allowed feelings of prejudice and elitism to linger in the first place.

One of the most salient features of stigma is fear. But today, we fear different attributes than our twentieth-century predecessors did. Instead of fearing unfamiliar races, nations, or religions, people in a more individualistic and egalitarian world are hesitant to make moral judgments about others but we have no hesitation about showing an obsessive concern about the visible signs of our own marketability, such as personal hygiene, physical fitness, health, and sexual attractiveness. We increasingly focus, therefore, on medical risks rather than moral risks. As Alan Wolfe has argued, "When nonjudgmental people make judgments, they often defer to the scientific and medical authorities whom they cite in avoiding making judgments in other situations."[7] Wolfe explores the ways that we medicalize our moral judgments—cloaking our opposition to smoking in the purported health risks of secondhand smoke rather than in our disapproval of the smoker's lack of self-control, for example—and the ways that we try to explain away our moral disapproval of self-destructive behavior by chalking it up to addiction rather than choice. In contrast to the moralistic Victorian era, Wolfe suggests, America has "entered a new era in which virtue and vice are redefined in terms of public health and addiction." Smoking and obesity are attacked as symbols of a failure of discipline that used to be associated with a failure of moral character.[8] And conditions or diseases that are feared to be contagious may lead the tainted individuals or places to be stigmatized with a ruthlessness that the ancient Greeks would have recognized.

Today, individuals and objects can become stigmatized not merely because they are infected with a contagious disease, but because they are symbolically contaminated in a way that others fear might be contagious. Paul Rozin of the University of Pennsylvania has studied the ways that fear of contagion can lead individuals to avoid even the briefest contact with an object that poses no actual health risk. Rozin gives the following example: You are about to drink a glass of juice, when a friend drops a cockroach in it. You refuse to drink it, on the grounds that cockroaches are dirty and might carry disease. The friend pours a new glass of juice and drops a dead sterilized cockroach into it, ensuring that there is no longer a safety issue. You refuse to drink again, confessing that the drink has been spoiled because it has been "cockroached" by brief contact with a disgusting object: What motivates you to spurn the juice is not a rational fear of disease, but a visceral reaction that is best described as being grossed out. The health risk turns out to be a masquerade for a psychological aversion that is harder to justify in rational terms.

The response to the cockroach, Rozin argues, illustrates what he calls "the law of contagion."[9] Because we respond more emotionally to negative than positive images, even the briefest physical contact with an object that is perceived to be contaminated can lead a person or an object to be perceived as contaminated as well. Once an object or a person has been spoiled or stigmatized, it may be very hard to remove the stigma: The cockroached juice remains objectionable even if the cockroach has been sterilized. And if there are psychological or moral fears lurking behind a medicalized fear, no amount of reassurance about physical risks will remove the stigma: This is why there is widespread reluctance to touch people with AIDS. The result may be the permanent shunning of individuals who are not, in fact, contagious but who engage our deep and ineradicable fears of contagion, which are rooted in a disgust that we dare not publicly express.

After 9/11, the most dramatic illustration of the principle of contagion was America's response to fears of anthrax. Four letters containing anthrax were mailed to congressional and media leaders in October 2001, leading to twenty-three cases of anthrax infections and five deaths by the end of November. But the disruption that resulted was wildly disproportionate to the actual risk: The Hart Senate Office Building was closed for months and decontaminated at a cost of $22 million. After traces of anthrax were found in its mailroom, the U.S. Supreme Court evacuated its courtroom for the first time since the building opened in 1935, and held a special session down the street at the U.S. Court of Appeals for the D.C. Circuit. When traces of spores were found at almost two dozen off-site mail facilities that served federal buildings throughout Washington, including the White House, the CIA, and the State Department and the Justice Department, mail to all federal government offices was shipped to Ohio to be decontaminated, delaying its delivery for months. The postmaster general told Congress that the total cost of the anthrax attacks could exceed $5 billion.[10]

After the anthrax attacks, many citizens reported increased levels of fear. During the month of October, the FBI investigated 2,500 reports of suspected anthrax attacks, many of which turned out to involve harmless substances such as talcum powder. There was a surge in purchases of gas masks and Cipro, the anthrax antibiotic. Three out of ten people surveyed in a Gallup Poll at the end of October said they had thought about buying a gas mask or Cipro, and more than half said they were considering handling their mail more cautiously.[11] In another poll, half said they had some concern about contracting anthrax, although the other half had little or no concern.[12] More than a third of Americans reported washing their hands after opening Christmas cards.[13] Whether this behavior should be interpreted as a limited panic by an irrational minority or as "reluctance to panic"[14] by the calmer majority is open to debate; but it demonstrates a level of concern vastly disproportionate to the actual threat of infection.

More striking than the fluctuating polls were the rituals that the government adopted in order to expunge the stigma of a mail system that had been tainted in just the way that Rozin's experiments with cockroaches suggest. Once the postal service had been marked in the public mind as a bearer of contamination, even the most remote possibility of contact with a letter that had passed through one of the facilities where a few anthrax spores had been detected became a source of public fear and disgust. Soon after the attacks, on the advice of the Centers for Disease Control and Prevention, universities and other private employers advised their employees to wash their hands after handling mail and to wear latex gloves when opening envelopes. Months after the attacks, the post office adopted elaborate procedures for the permanent irradiation, in off-site facilities, of letters addressed to federal offices, resulting in substantial delays. And a post office report issued in March 2002 promised to implement a "multi-layered, multi-year Emergency Preparedness Plan" to protect customers and employees from exposure to biohazardous material and safeguard the mail system from future attacks. The plan includes the deployment of technology to identify and track all retail mail in the United States; to scan each letter for possible contamination; to sanitize mail addressed to targeted groups; and to expand the use of "e-beam and X-ray irradiation" of contaminated mail. It aspires in the next few years to develop an "intelligent mail system" that would allow "capturing and retaining data to enable tracking and tracing of mail items, data mining to allow forensic investigation, and positive product tracking to eliminate anonymous mail." Within four years of its implementation, the program is estimated to cost up to $2.4 billion a year.[15]

Recall that these extraordinary rituals, which have permanently changed the way mail is delivered in America, were triggered by an attack that claimed only five lives. But the rituals were designed not to purify the mail but to eliminate the stigma that has attached itself to the American postal system. Like the early Christians who understood stigmata as bodily signs of holy grace, and thus transformed the symbols of Christ's ultimate sacrifice into symbols of divine favor, we are attempting to purge the stigma of anthrax by reenacting a ritual of reassurance. In this sense, the scanning of envelopes for anthrax is similar to the rituals that require us to remove our shoes at the airport or to use plastic knives in the sky. Like a religious rite, its purpose is psychological rather than empirical. Just as people take Communion to remind themselves that Jesus died on the Cross and sacrificed Himself for their sins, so people remove their shoes to give themselves the illusion of being protected from future shoe bombers. Like believers taking the leap of faith, they are more concerned about ritualized expressions of safety than about safety itself.

Our response to the anthrax attacks after 9/11 is only one example of the tendency of crowds to think in terms of emotional images rather than reasoned arguments, which helps to explain why different groups respond differently to unfamiliar risks. In a Gallup Poll taken soon after September 11, 69 percent of the women surveyed said they were "very worried" that their families might be victimized by terrorist attacks. Only 46 percent of the men were similarly concerned. Paul Slovic's work suggests that in thinking about a range of risks—from the hazards of nuclear waste to the possibility of being victimized by crime and violence—men tend to judge the risks as smaller and less threatening than women.[16] Better educated, richer people perceive themselves to be less at risk than their poorer counterparts. People of color tend to be more fearful of risk than white people. And white men consistently perceive risks to be lower than everyone else, including white women and men and women of color.

When Slovic examined the data more closely, however, he found that not all white men are less fearful than everyone else. The "white male effect," he discovered, seemed to be caused by about 30 percent of the white men surveyed, who judged risks to be extremely low. The rest of the white men didn't perceive risks very differently from all the other groups.[17] What distinguished the 30 percent of less fearful white men from everyone else? They shared certain characteristics that had more to do with their worldview than with their sex. The calmer white men tended to be less egalitarian than everyone else: A majority agreed with the proposition that America has gone too far in pursuing equal rights. They tended to display more trust in authorities, agreeing that government and industry could be relied on to manage technological risks. By wide margins, they felt very much in control of risks to their own health, and they agreed that if a risk was small, society could impose it on other individuals without their consent. They believed that individuals should be able to take care of themselves. In short, they were more politically conservative, more hierarchical, more trusting of authority, and less egalitarian than most of their fellow Americans.

One reason that relatively conservative white men seem to be less concerned about risk than their fellow citizens is that people are most fearful of risks they perceive as beyond their ability to control. Many Americans preferred to drive rather than to fly in the months following September 11, even though their risks of being killed in a car crash were greater than their risks of being killed in another terrorist attack. At the wheel of a car, people have an illusion of control that they can't achieve as passengers on a plane, and, therefore, they tend to underestimate the risk of driving and overestimate the risk of flying. It isn't easy to imagine yourself in situations you haven't personally experienced, which means that people have a hard time making decisions about unfamiliar and remote risks. This is why people fear most being a victim of those crimes that they are, in fact, least likely to experience. Women worry most about violent crime, even though they have the lowest risk of being victims, while young men worry the least, even though they have the highest risk. Because of their physical differences, men have a greater illusion of control over their ability to respond to violent crime than women do. In areas where women feel more in control than men, however, they are more likely to engage in risky behavior. When it comes to social risks—such as asking strangers for directions—women turn out to be more intrepid than men. Because men are more reluctant than women to risk the humiliation of appearing foolish before strangers, they perceive the ordeal to be more socially risky.

In the case of terrorism after 9/11, in fact, men and women appear to be equally at risk. But the best explanation for why men perceive the risk of future terrorist attacks to be lower than women do is that men tend to be angrier than women about the 9/11 attacks, while women tend to be more fearful. In a study of 1,000 Americans conducted a few weeks after 9/11, a group of scholars at Carnegie Mellon University found that women believed they had a greater chance of being hurt in a future terrorist attack than men did. Eighty-one percent of the difference between men's and women's perception of risk could be explained by the fact that women reported lower degrees of anger about the attacks, and higher degrees of fear.[18] Fear is more likely to arise in people who feel uncertain and unable to control future events, while anger is more likely to arise in people who are more confident of their ability to control their environment. Because angrier people have a greater sense of personal control than fearful ones, they tend to be less pessimistic about the possibility of future attacks.

Despite these gender differences, both men and women dramatically overestimated the risks of a future attack after 9/11: The respondents saw a 20 percent chance that they would be personally hurt in a terrorist attack within the next year, and a nearly 50 percent chance that the average American would be hurt. Thankfully, these predictions proved to be wrong, and there was no attack comparable to those on the World Trade Center in the twelve months following 9/11. But the predictions seemed alarmist even when they were made: They could have come true only if an attack of similar magnitude occurred nearly every day for the following year. This shows how liable people are to exaggerate the risk of terrorism because of their tendency to evaluate probabilities in emotional rather than empirical terms.

Behavioral economists and psychologists have found that in making decisions about unfamiliar events, people rely on mental shortcuts, or heuristics, that often lead them to miscalculate the probability of especially dreaded hazards. People believe that they are most likely to be victimized by the threats of which they are most afraid. They imagine that they are more likely to be harmed by nuclear accidents, terrorism, and radioactive pollution than by less dreaded accidents involving power mowers, railroads, or skiing, even though the less dreaded accidents are, in fact, more likely to occur. Terrorism, in this regard, is among the risks that are so horrific to contemplate and hard to control that people's judgments about its probability are likely to be especially clouded by their fear of the outcome. Acts of terrorism are dreaded in the extreme: Their effects are inequitably distributed, they unfairly burden victims without any compensating benefits, and they are hard to predict and hard to understand. This means that relatively minor acts of terrorism can cause fear that greatly exceeds the immediate injuries they cause or the probability that they will recur.

One reason that people have difficulty coolly appraising the risks of especially frightening threats reflects a phenomenon that Slovic calls the "affect heuristic"—that is, the tendency of people to make judgments about risk based on emotional feelings and intuitions about whether something is good or bad, rather than on a dispassionate calculation of costs and benefits. Affective judgments are holistic rather than analytic; they focus on pleasure and pain rather than logic, on free associations rather than deductive connections. They take the form of images, metaphors, and narratives—all of which are deeply embedded in our therapeutic and democratic culture—rather than of abstract symbols, words, and numbers. They justify themselves— on the theory that "experiencing is believing"—rather than requiring justification by logic and evidence.[19] In evaluating the risk of flying, for example, people don't tally up the number of plane accidents versus auto accidents; instead, they ask themselves broadly whether they like airplanes, whether they feel comfortable in them, and whether they think they are safe and good. Because our judgments about risks and benefits are guided by seat-of-the-pants emotional impressions about whether we like or dislike an activity, all things considered, we tend not to be swayed by empirical evidence. This makes us especially vulnerable to overestimating the risks of hazards that we fear, even when experts tell us to calm down.

The tendency of crowds to make judgments about risks based on visual images rather than on reasoned arguments results in another mental shortcut that leads us to overestimate the probability of especially dramatic risks. People fixate on the hazards that catch their attention, which means those that are easiest to imagine and recall. As Gustave Le Bon recognized in *The Crowd*, a single memorable image will crowd out less visually dramatic risks in the public mind and will lead people wrongly to imagine that they are more likely to be victims of terrorism than of mundane risks, like heart disease. The Nobel Prize winners Amos Tversky and Daniel Kahneman have called this the "availability heuristic,"[20] which they define as the tendency to assume that an event is likely to recur if examples of it are easy to remember. We saw examples of this phenomenon in chapter 1, where a single vivid image of a two-year-old boy being led off to his doom by his ten-year-old assailants, replayed constantly on British television, caused fear of child abductions to spike in Britain, and led to the installment of CCTV cameras, even though British children were more likely to be killed by exploding air bags than by prepubescent kidnappers. For the same reason, people overestimate the frequency of deaths from dramatic disasters such as tornadoes, floods, fire, and homicide and underestimate the frequency of deaths from diabetes, stomach cancer, stroke, and asthma.[21]

When presented with two estimations of risk—one high and the other low—people tend to believe the high risk estimation regardless of whether it comes from government or industry.[22] This bias toward the worst-case scenario is another example of the fact that crowds, when their emotions are intensely engaged, tend to focus on the vividness of a particularly unpleasant risk rather than on its likelihood. This phenomenon, which Cass Sunstein calls "probability neglect,"[23] can lead to behavioral changes that strike experts as irrational, such as buying gas masks and Cipro and canceling flights while continuing to drive and eat Big Macs. The print and electronic media play an important role in contributing to this behavior, but it is a role that can't be separated from the demands of the public itself. Most journalists can tell stories of editors who have pressured them to describe worst-case scenarios, in order to scare the au-

dience into thinking that the story in question is somehow relevant to their lives. As Tocqueville noted in his discussion of
why American writers are bombastic, citizens in democratic societies spend most of their time contemplating themselves, and
can be tempted to stop gazing at their navels only when they
are confronted with the largest and most gripping of subjects.
Writers, therefore, have an incentive to attract the attention of
the crowd by exaggerating the significance of every topic: If
they report that things aren't as bad as they might be, the public won't pay attention. Because of this unfortunate dynamic,
Tocqueville reported, "the author and the public corrupt one
another at the same time."[24]

When reporting on essentially random risks, there is especially great pressure on reporters to exaggerate the scope and
probability of the danger, in order to make more people feel
that they, too, could be victims. Joel Best of Southern Illinois
University has examined the "moral panics" about dramatic
new crimes that seized the public attention in the 1980s and
1990s, such as freeway violence in 1987, wilding in 1989,
stalking around 1990, children and guns in 1991, and so forth.
In each of these cases, Best writes, the television media seized
on two or three incidents of a dramatic crime, such as freeway
shooting, and then claimed that it was part of a broader trend.
By taking the worst and most infrequent examples of criminal
violence and melodramatically claiming they were typical, TV
created the impression that everyone was at risk, thereby increasing its audience. Although the idea of random violence appeals to our democratic sensibilities—if violence is random,
then everyone is equally at risk—Best points out that "most
violence is not patternless, is not pointless, nor is it increasing

in the uncontrolled manner we imagine."[25] After purported trends failed to pan out in most of the cases described above, the media spotlight moved on in search of new and even more melodramatic threats.

Exaggerated reports of violence on television appear to distort people's fears of violence in daily life. A survey of prime-time-television viewing by George Gerbner, former dean of the Annenberg School at the University of Pennsylvania, found that heavy TV watchers are more likely than lighter ones to overestimate their chances of being involved in violence, to believe that their neighborhood is unsafe, to say that fear of crime is a very serious problem, to assume that crime is rising even when it is falling, and to buy locks, watchdogs, and guns for protection.[26] And this distortion isn't limited to television. Jason Ditton of the University of Sheffield notes that 45 percent of crimes reported in the newspaper involve sex or violence, compared with only 3 percent of reported crime. When people were interviewed about how many crimes involve sex or violence, they tended to overestimate it by a factor of three. People fear being assaulted or raped more than being robbed, even though there is a higher incidence of robbery than rape.

After 9/11, the media's focus on worst-case scenarios had predictable effects. The most respectable magazines and newspapers ran a series of dire articles imagining how the nation would fare under nuclear or biochemical attacks.[27] These stories took their toll. A study of psychological responses to 9/11 found that, two months after the attacks, 17 percent of the U.S. population outside of New York City reported symptoms of post-traumatic stress related to 9/11. (This number fell to 6 percent after six months.) High levels of stress were especially notable in women, those with a previous history of depression or anxiety disorders, and those who watched a lot of television. Nearly half of the respondents reported watching more than four hours of television a day in the weeks following the attacks, and these heavy TV watchers were far more likely to be anxious than citizens with more temperate viewing habits.[28]

The television and print media are not the only influences on public opinion that have an incentive to exaggerate risks in the hope of attracting an audience. After 9/11, we learned that politicians had an additional incentive to pass along vague and unconfirmed threats of future violence, in order to protect themselves from criticism in the event that another attack materialized. The attorney general's proclivity for announcing periodically that a future terrorist attack was "likely," without providing further details about how the danger could be minimized, did not contribute to public calm. Nor did the twenty-four-hour alarmist banners on cable TV or the director of homeland security's color-coded terrorist-threat-level warning system.

Before 9/11, many symbolic and ineffective laws were passed to reassure a skittish public in the wake of highly publicized but low-probability disasters. A few shark attacks in the summer of 2001 led to lurid media reports of the "summer of the shark," even though there was no evidence that shark attacks were on the rise. In response to public pressure, a Florida commission banned shark feeding.[29] A few highly publicized child abductions in the late 1990s led state legislatures to pass more than fifty laws over an eighteen-month period with names like Amber's Law in Texas and Jenna's Law in New York that punished child abductors with Caligulan severity.[30] After a handful of women told emotional stories on television of being injured by silicone breast implants, the U.S. Food and Drug Administration restricted the use of implants in 1992, although there was no reliable medical evidence that the implants caused health problems.[31] In each case, the laws remained in place after the attention of the public had drifted to another melodramatic panic, but because few people are inclined to feed sharks or to abduct children, the ineffectiveness of the laws was largely ignored.

In addition to being ineffective, laws passed in the wake of highly publicized, visually memorable attacks tend to strike unfortunate balances between liberty and security, failing to ensure that the most draconian searches, seizures, and punishments are reserved for the most serious crimes. In the USA Patriot Act, for example, Congress expanded federal authority to investigate all crimes, not just terrorist crimes. Similarly, in the 1990s, laws adopted after the Oklahoma City bombing and the murders of Polly Klaas and Megan Kanka expanded law enforcement authority to investigate a broad class of offenses, not just those that inspired their passage. In 2003, the Supreme Court rejected constitutional challenges to all three of these laws—challenges that argued, in different ways, that the punishments they imposed were disproportionate to the crimes in question.[32] But because there is no clear constitutional requirement of proportionality, most of these laws, like the USA Patriot Act, will remain on the books long after the crises that provoked them have been forgotten.

After 9/11, the public demand for laws that promise to provide complete security against remote but visually memorable risks was brought home with a vengeance to travelers at every airport in the nation. In a ritualistic attempt to expunge the taint of its most visible security failure, the Federal Aviation Administration imposed a series of regulations requiring all travelers to divest themselves of any personal implements that resembled the box cutters used by the World Trade Center hijackers. Millions of travelers experienced the pointless indignity of surrendering their toenail clippers and of having their toiletry kits scoured for grooming scissors. Once on board, all travelers were forced to eat with plastic knives but were allowed the indulgence of metal forks. These regulations were designed not to disarm passengers of every conceivable weapon—a determined terrorist remained free to create a makeshift rapier out of a broken mini-bottle of Chardonnay. Instead they were designed to calm nervous passengers who remained transfixed by images of terrorists brandishing box cutters. So zealously was the zero-risk mentality pursued that entire airports were closed down if a single nail clipper was mistakenly allowed to slip past the security guards.

Like many Americans, my wife and I experienced the foolishness of these rules. After landing at Dulles Airport in Washington, our plane was forced to languish on the runway for two hours. The official explanation was that there had been a security emergency, but it emerged in the papers the next day that a backpacking student had inadvertently passed through the security area with a three-inch penknife and then disappeared into the crowd. Five thousand passengers were evacuated and delayed for hours as everyone was forced to go through security again, in an attempt to find the bewildered backpacker.[33] Instead of being indignant about this disruptive ritual, however, many people accepted it because it made them feel better.

"It's for our safety," one placid traveler told the local news as she waited in line for hours, in a contented echo of the British mantra about surveillance cameras.

Nevertheless, the rituals of security continue to proliferate. Three months after 9/11, a new image seized the imagination of the nation when Richard C. Reid, a British citizen, was thwarted during a flight from Paris to Miami in the middle of an attempt to ignite the fuse of a bomb that he had concealed in one of his black high-top sneakers. New federal regulations quickly followed requiring randomly selected travelers to take off their shoes at airport checkpoints and send them through metal detectors. It is now commonplace to see frail old ladies frisked like street hoodlums, their high-heeled shoes at their sides and their arms spread helplessly as they are wanded by uniformed guards. This indignity serves no security purpose, but it does serve a civic purpose. It is designed to remind American travelers, in the most visible and dramatic way possible, of the country's unshakable commitment to equality. When confronted with a choice between giving airline authorities discretion to single out the most suspicious looking travelers, which raises the specter of discrimination, and subjecting the least-threatening travelers to a demeaning and ineffective ordeal, the government has chosen equality rather than liberty or security.

This commitment to equality, above all, often requires absurd public rituals of shared inconvenience, as a symbol of the government's determination to eradicate low-probability risks that can't, in fact, be eliminated. Low-probability risks, after all, are the most dramatic offenses against equality: They strike without warning and single out from the crowd an unlucky few who are made to endure calamities that everyone else is spared. In *The Gilded Age,* published in 1873, Mark Twain described a steamship accident that killed twenty-two people. The verdict in that less egalitarian age: "Nobody to Blame."[34] In the twentieth century, by contrast, America developed what the legal historian Lawrence Friedman has called a pervasive expectation of "total justice," as well as the related expectation "that somebody will pay for any and all calamities that happen to a person, provided only that it is not the victim's 'fault,' or at least not solely his fault."[35] The expectations of total justice and total recompense manifest themselves in the legalization of risk—the effort to compensate individuals for every misfortune, social slight, or general brush with unfairness or bad luck. They are reflected in the elimination of legal doctrines like assumption of risk, which held that people shouldn't be compensated for accidents whose risks they should have understood. Since 9/11, the most egregious display of this total-justice mentality has been the decision by a group of trial lawyers to sue the architects of the World Trade Center on behalf of the victims' families. Their claim: The Twin Towers should have been better designed to withstand a terrorist attack. Later in the year, 600 relatives of victims of the 9/11 attacks filed a lawsuit for $1 trillion aimed at international banks who purportedly (if unwittingly) aided the terrorists. If someone has to pay for every misfortune, why not begin by going after those who can afford it?

In negotiating the uncertainties of identity in modern society, individuals must devote a great deal of energy not only to anticipating future risks, but also in deciding whom to trust. In traditional societies, trust can arise from personal relationships and family structures; in modern societies, where these markers have atrophied, individuals increasingly rely for their security on strangers and impersonal experts. This makes the question of which strangers and experts to trust especially urgent. Paul Slovic's research suggests that people's willingness to accept risk is directly linked to how much they trust the authorities in charge of managing the risk. People view medical technologies that rely on radiation and chemicals—such as X-ray machines and prescription drugs—as being low in risk and high in benefit, while they view industrial technologies that rely on radiation and chemicals—such as nuclear power and pesticides—as being high in risk and low in benefit. They are willing to overlook the significant risks posed by X-rays and medicines because they trust the physicians who manage the medical technologies more than they trust the government and industry officials who manage the industrial technologies.[36] We don't worry about wild animals escaping from the zoo because we trust zookeepers, but we do worry about the nuclear waste escaping from a secure burying ground in the desert because we don't trust nuclear engineers. Moreover, trust in particular authorities is constantly undermined by the same vicious cycle I discussed earlier, in which politicians, the media, interest groups, and an adversarial legal system all have incentives to encourage an already mistrustful public to exaggerate risks. To the degree that "the system destroys trust,"[37] as Slovic puts it, a society becomes even less able to endure the uncertainties posed by unfamiliar risks.

If a more egalitarian, individualistic, antiauthoritarian society like America is more likely to fear low-probability risks, a less egalitarian, less individualistic, more hierarchical society should be less fearful. And this, more or less, is what the evidence suggests: A comparative study of risk perception in the United States and France revealed that the French saw greater economic benefits from nuclear power and a greater need for it. This difference in attitude reflected the fact that the French had greater trust in the scientists and officials from government and industry who designed and regulated the plants, and they also were more likely than the Americans to believe that regulatory authority should be entrusted to experts and government officials rather than to the people.[38] In this (and perhaps only this) sense, the French were like the 30 percent of American white men who turned out to be more conservative, less egalitarian, and more trusting of authority than their more skittish fellow citizens.

In countries where the public is inclined to be suspicious of experts, the experts respond by pandering to the public, further inflaming the fears they should dispassionately assess. Bill Durodié of Oxford University has discussed the degradation of risk analysis in democratic societies as scientists and government officials feel increasing pressure to emphasize the uncertainties rather than the potential benefits of risky products and events. Public opinion, which abhors elitism above all, demands that experts today show more humility than their confident predecessors and incorporate folk wisdom and popular values into their analyses of risk. The result of these democratic pressures on scientific objectivity has been "the precautionary principle," which suggests that "in the absence of definitive scientific evidence to the contrary, measures to protect the environment or human health should be taken whenever any threat of serious or irreversible damage to either may be present,"[39] no matter how remote. "The precautionary principle has the consequence of emphasizing worst case scenarios," Durodié argues, "thereby encouraging a tendency to overreact to events and, more insidiously, elevating public opinion over professional expertise and subordinating science to prejudice."[40] He points to the British scientific establishment's response to the hysteria over mad cow disease.

Mad cow disease was first detected in British cattle in 1986. For the next decade, the British government and scientific establishment argued that the available evidence suggested no connection between mad cow disease and a degenerative brain disorder in humans known as Creutzfeldt-Jakob disease, or CJD. But in 1995, the deaths of two British teenagers from CJD created rising public panic; the BBC reported that a quarter of Britons were eating less beef, based on fears that mad cow disease could infect people.[41] In December 1995, the leading brain-disease expert told the BBC that he would not eat a hamburger "under any circumstances," because there was growing evidence that CJD could be caught from infected beef, although he provided no evidence.[42] The following March, the British health secretary told the House of Commons that the government couldn't rule out a link between mad cow disease and CJD. This announcement led to a global ban on the consumption of British beef, a drop in beef consumption by 11 percent across the European Union, and a cost to Britain of more than £4 billion.

In fact, the panic bore little relation to any immediate threat: The British government had stemmed the mad cow epidemic as early as 1988, and the incidents of mad cow disease fell from nearly 37,000 in 1987 to 1 in 1996, which was the year the panic took hold.[43] Nevertheless, in 2000, a government commission that had been convened to evaluate the scientific evidence equivocated in the face of lingering public concern. Acknowledging the lack of conclusive evidence of a link between mad cow disease and CJD, the commission concluded weakly that "the importance of precautionary measures should not be played down on the grounds that the risk is unproven."[44] The commission also went out of its way to recognize the pain of the families of the victims of CJD, whose tragic personal stories contributed few insights about preventing the disease. In its emphasis on sentiment rather than scientific evidence, the commission seemed more concerned about acknowledging the persistent fears of the public than about telling the British people that they had been seized by a mass panic. And by careening from initial claims that there was no risk to inflated claims of significant risk, the scientists further undermined whatever trust in their expertise the anxious public may have had in the first place, and this undermining of trust further inflamed the public's anxieties. Durodié quotes the Slovian philosopher Slavoj Zizek on behalf of the proposition that "endless precautions" and "incessant procrastination" are characteristic of "the obsessional neurotic,"[45] and indeed there is a neurotic element to Britain's response to its fears of mad cow disease: Unwilling to defer to any expert who refused to confirm its unsupported prejudices, the crowd rewarded the scientists who were willing to flatter its obsessions by cheering it on to self-justifying waves of alarm.

Slovic insists that the public's reliance on emotions and intuitions rather than on a cool weighing of probabilities should not be dismissed out of hand. Risk, he insists, is a subjective concept whose accuracy is often hard to evaluate. If the question is how afraid we should be of a dirty bomb, for example, people will disagree about how to weigh the different values at stake. Some will focus more on the remote probability of a catastrophic accident in their neighborhood and others on the potential severity. Some will be more concerned about the possibility that children might be exposed and others will be more concerned about themselves. There is, he insists, a "rival rationality" that risk analysts sometimes leave out of their calculations of costs and benefits: Because people in a pluralistic democracy have different values that will color their definitions of risk, the question of who gets to define risk is itself an exercise of power that can't be entirely delegated to experts. Everyone, in short, should have a say.

Be that as it may, the various mental shortcuts that Slovic has identified suggest that people will be especially bad at evaluating laws and technologies and risks that require them to balance competing values in cases where the emotional images associated with one of the values are easier to remember and more emotionally gripping than the images of the other. In evaluating competing values, people weigh vivid and memorable images more heavily than diffuse and imprecise ones. They don't jump at the chance to room with an intelligent and obnoxious roommate, for example, because intelligence, while a positive trait, doesn't create warm and fuzzy images of likability, while obnoxiousness produces a precise and memorable negative impression.[46] In evaluations of airline security measures, Slovic found that people are more likely to support a safety measure expected to save 98 percent of the 150 lives at risk than a measure expected to save 150 lives.[47] This is because 98 percent is much easier to remember and a more precise image than the vague and diffuse figure of 150.

The same zero-risk mentality influences the way people approach technological responses to terrorism. In a survey of Harvard students after 9/11, W. Kip Viscusi and Richard Zeckhauser found that people were willing to pay disproportionately more for technologies that promise to eliminate the risk of terrorism than for technologies that promise to reduce the risk without eliminating it. Asked how much they would pay for airport screening technologies that scanned luggage and passengers, the respondents in the Harvard survey were willing to pay more than twice as much for a technology that would reduce the risk to zero than they were willing to pay for a technology that would reduce the risk by 50 percent. These findings are consistent with many other studies that have found that promises of risk elimination receive far more public support than promises of risk reduction. "This zero risk mentality is usually viewed as a form of irrationality though there could be possible rational explanations for it, such as the elimination of anxiety with respect to a non-zero level of risk," the Harvard study notes.[48]

Relying on feelings to calculate risks often leads people to make all-or-nothing, snap judgments that are often wrong: They assume that risky activities like smoking and drinking alcohol have low benefits, and beneficial activities like being administered vaccines and being X-rayed have low risks.[49] In fact, many activities can be both risky and beneficial (unprotected sex, for example), or low in both risks and benefits (such as watching reality TV). When presented with promises that a particular technology is beneficial, people may conclude that it poses few risks, and vice versa, even if there is no logical correlation between the promised benefit and the threatened risk. Furthermore, loss aversion theory predicts that people tend to be risk-averse when choosing a benefit but risk-takers when avoiding a loss. When choosing between avoiding sure and unsure losses, people tend to avoid the sure loss.[50] This all-or-nothing emotionalism means that people may not be well equipped to evaluate technologies and laws that ask them to make trade-offs between privacy and security. Security is an emotionally gripping value—when coupled with terrifying images of terrorist attacks, it's something that people want immediately. Also, the losses associated with terrorism are certain and sure. By contrast, privacy, liberty, and equality are more amorphous—their benefits are diffuse and the costs of losing them are uncertain and hard to visualize. It shouldn't be a surprise, therefore, that the English people have fallen over themselves in embracing a surveillance technology like security cameras. When told that the cameras have immediate and dramatic benefits in reducing crime, people will naturally assume that they pose low risks to privacy. ("Nothing to hide, nothing to fear.") The fact that the cameras make people feel safe is more important than the empirical studies suggesting that they don't, in fact, decrease crime. In a world of emotion and images, the feeling of safety justifies itself.

It's arguable, of course, that even feel-good security measures have psychological benefits whether or not they make people safer. Perhaps those benefits—which could include increased workplace efficiency, consumer confidence, and economic stability—might justify the cost of ineffective security measures that make people feel safe without, in fact, making them safe. But given the reality of the terrorists threats that menace us, and the tremendous psychological and economic costs of future attacks, it seems more plausible to conclude that the money would be better spent on well-designed anti-terrorist measures that could save more lives at a lower cost.[51]

The reluctance of the public to make nuanced judgments in the face of remote threats, however, has made it hard to find a market demand for well-designed technologies that protect liberty and security at the same time. In the private sector, there is a degree of consumer demand for control over personal information. Ann Cavoukian, the energetic privacy commissioner of Ontario, Canada, notes that before 9/11, a growing number of companies—including IBM, EarthLink, Hewlett-Packard, the Royal Bank of Canada, and Expedia—had discovered the financial benefits of making consumer privacy a business priority. The Royal Bank of Canada, the largest financial institution in that country, found that privacy accounted for 14 percent of its overall brand value and 7 percent of the economic value to shareholders.[52] Along the same lines, in 2000, EarthLink, the Internet service provider, became one of the first companies to appoint a chief privacy officer, and it went out of its way to promote the benefits of anonymous Web browsing and e-mail without spam. In September 2001, it found that in cities where it emphasized its respect for privacy, its business had jumped by 70 percent.[53]

Then, of course, came 9/11. But although the terrorist attacks were followed by increased trust in government, they did not inspire increased trust in business's ability to handle personal information: In a consumer survey, the privacy consultant Alan Westin found that 76 percent of his respondents said that their concerns about privacy hadn't changed after 9/11, while 22 percent said that privacy was even more important.[54] As a sign of the continued salience of the issue, a month after the attacks, IBM announced the creation of a privacy research institute, designed to fund research on long-term privacy and technology projects. And the following year, more than twelve months after the attacks, Bill Gates wrote a memo to Microsoft employees called "Trustworthy Computing," in which he called security and privacy the "highest priority" for Microsoft's new Web strategy, known as .Net.

The IBM Privacy Research Institute is only one of several research centers focused on the development of privacy-enhancing technologies, or PETs, which seek to protect consumer privacy by minimizing or eliminating the use of data that can be linked to identifiable individuals. As Ann Cavoukian notes, PETs in the business sphere include digital cash and other transactions based on blind digital signatures, which allow electronic communications to be authenticated without revealing the identities of the people behind them; privacy-management technologies such as audit features that carefully track the movement of personal data and record precisely who has accessed it; pseudonymous and anonymous Web-browsing technologies that allow individuals to mask their identities as they visit different sites; and onetime "disposable" credit cards that can help to prevent identity theft.[55]

For better or for worse, however, none of these privacy-enhancing technologies has found a market niche sufficiently large to make them commercially viable on their own. Given the choice between privacy and convenience, consumers tend to choose convenience in a pinch. And in the national security arena, choices about the trade-off between civil liberties and the reduction of risk also tend to be driven by concerns about efficiency. In their survey of Harvard students, Viscusi and Zeckhauser found that people's willingness to tolerate racial profiling of passengers other than themselves at airports depended on how much waiting time they themselves would save. Forty-five percent favored racial profiling when the alternative was for them to wait an extra ten minutes in line; these numbers rose to 55 percent if the delay was thirty minutes and 74 percent if the delay was an hour. In other words, nearly 30 percent were willing to tolerate racial profiling if it would save everyone an hour, but not if it would save only ten minutes. (African American respondents who had themselves been victimized by profiling were less willing to tolerate it for other people than were white respondents.)[56]

Privacy and equality, of course, are not absolute values; and there is nothing wrong with individuals making pragmatic judgments about the proper balance between liberty and security as long as they are getting something in return for the liberty they have surrendered. But the various biases in risk assessment that I've discussed—the affect and availability heuristics and the certainty premium associated with a zero-risk mentality—mean that people may not take the trouble to make a considered cost-benefit analysis. They may not demand an architecture (like the Blob Machine) that promises to protect privacy and security, preferring instead to settle for a similar but more invasive architecture (like the Naked Machine) that promises no more security but a greater feeling of safety.

In her capacity as the Ontario privacy commissioner, Ann Cavoukian has identified a series of what she calls STEPs, or "security technologies enabling privacy."[57] These include technologies like the Blob Machine, as well as sophisticated designs for surveillance cameras that can mask the identity of individuals unless there is a good reason to identify them. For example, Dutch researchers have invented something called PrivaCam that breaks up the digital video stream inside a surveillance camera into several data feeds. With access to only one feed, a viewer would have no idea what occurred at the scene; in order for the footage to be intelligible, several interested parties—such as the police, the property owner, and a neutral judge—would have to agree to put the feeds back together.[58] By keeping the feeds in separate places, the PrivaCam makes it more difficult for the images to be used for purposes unrelated to those for which they were originally recorded. Other possible technologies include the privacy-enhancing cameras developed by the IBM Privacy Research Institute that can block out the faces of individuals or the times and locations of particular events. The cameras can be programmed to alert law enforcement officials to suspicious movements without allowing them to identify suspects without approval from a judge or supervisor.[59] Although privacy-enhancing designs like the PrivaCam and the IBM alternative promise just as much security as the British CCTV cameras, the intentional inefficiencies they incorporate may make people *feel* less safe without making them less safe in fact. And since the feeling of safety is the most tangible benefit that the cameras can deliver, security technologies that enhance privacy may have a hard time finding a market in the anxious public square.

In the next chapter, I will argue that the choices represented by the Blob Machine and the Naked Machine, or the British

CCTV cameras and the Dutch PrivaCam, are ubiquitous. Nearly all the technologies of security now being developed by technologists and adapted by government can be designed in ways that strike a better or worse balance between liberty and security. But because the public may not demand technologies that protect privacy and liberty as well as security, the technologists may not build them on their own. For a vision of the strengths and weaknesses of a market-based approach to protecting liberty and security, let's turn next to Silicon Valley.

—

CHAPTER THREE

The Silver Bullet

GILMAN LOUIE IS ONE OF THE MOST SUCCESSFUL computer-game developers of all time. "I'm your classic entrepreneur," he says modestly. "I started my first business with my fraternity brothers at San Francisco State." Louie, an amateur fighter pilot, had his first big success in 1987 with a game called Falcon, which allowed players to simulate the flight of an F-16. Falcon sold millions of copies, not only to teenage boys but also to pilots in the United States Air Force, who found it so realistic that it helped them learn to fly real fighter jets. Louie's biggest triumph came in 1988, when he imported from the Soviet Union an unexpectedly addictive game called Tetris, which became the best-selling computer game ever. Many companies were impressed by Louie's success, including Hasbro, which put him in charge of creating its games Web site. And then in 1998, Louie was recruited by an even more powerful employer: the Central Intelligence Agency. "The CIA actually thought that my computer-game background was a valuable asset,"

Louie recalls. "I look at the world as one big system—one big game."

The CIA had just founded an unusual venture-capital firm called In-Q-Tel, and the agency wanted Louie to be the CEO. "The 'Q' stands for the 'Q' factor—it's named after the character in *James Bond*," says Louie. In-Q-Tel was the brainchild of George Tenet, the CIA director, who believed that by investing $30 million a year in Internet start-ups in Silicon Valley, the CIA could encourage the development of cutting-edge technologies that might be useful for national intelligence. Louie's marching orders were to provide venture capital for data-mining technologies that would allow the CIA to monitor and profile potential terrorists as closely and carefully as Amazon monitors and profiles potential customers.

Silicon Valley has long indulged its own antiestablishment mythology, and Louie was worried that persuading programmers to collaborate with the CIA would be "borderline ludicrous." Despite his doubts, Louie agreed to open one In-Q-Tel office in Menlo Park, California, and another near Washington, D.C. He quickly discovered that far from recoiling at the idea of working with the CIA, Internet entrepreneurs flocked to his door. After the dot-com crash, high-tech entrepreneurs, desperate for venture capital, began to depend more and more on the federal government, and Silicon Valley tried to reinvent itself as the headquarters of the military-technological complex. Then came 9/11, and the establishment of the Office of Homeland Security. In-Q-Tel found itself to be just one of several deep-pocketed, federally financed investors eager to back technological solutions to our new security challenges. In 2002, the

Bush administration asked Congress for $38 billion for home-land security, and much of this money was to be parceled out among competing federal agencies—including the Defense Department and the FBI—which could then use the money either to invest directly in security technologies or to follow In-Q-Tel's model of providing venture capital to young companies in the private sector. Like the CIA, the Office of Homeland Security and the Justice Department concluded that the same technologies that were useful before 9/11 for tracking, profiling, and targeting potential customers could be turned after 9/11 on potential terrorists. "If Johnson & Johnson can use these technologies to sell soap," Viet Dinh, the former assistant attorney general, said, "we should be able to use them to fight terrorism."

As entrepreneurs flocked from California to Washington, the technologies of identification continued to proliferate. There were biometric identification devices, including hand scanners, iris scanners, and thumbprint, fingerprint, and handwriting scanners, that could pick strangers out of a crowd; ID cards, smart cards, and "trusted traveler cards," proposed by the airlines as a way of allowing prescreened passengers to pass more quickly through security; virtual links between masses of decentralized databases, making it possible for federal agencies to share personal information about citizens and aliens and to analyze and classify the risk posed by each traveler; brain wave scanners that could be deployed at airports to see whether a passenger was lying; data-mining and data-profiling technologies that promised to solve the "Tower of Babel problem," which results from the difficulty of converting vast amounts of decentralized data into usable intelligence; geospatial search engines, described as a combination of the search engine Google and "Mapquest on steroids,"[1] that could search the Web, identify where particular information was located, and identify unusual patterns; and tiny sensors that could be placed in the subway and identify molecular changes in the air, providing early warning of a nuclear, chemical, or biological attack. Giddy with all the possibilities, the president and Congress proved to be enthusiastic supporters of the search for technological silver bullets in the war on terrorism. "New technologies for analysis, information sharing, detection of attacks, and countering chemical, biological, radiological, and nuclear weapons will help prevent and minimize the damage from future terrorist attacks," declared the president's report on homeland security. "Just as science and technology have helped us defeat past enemies overseas, so too will they help us defeat the efforts of terrorists to attack our homeland and disrupt our way of life."[2]

In this spirit, the high-tech research office of the Department of Defense created a program called "Total Information Awareness," the most sweeping effort to monitor the activities of Americans since the government proposed a national data center in 1965. Directed by John Poindexter, former national security adviser to President Reagan, whose conviction for lying to Congress was overturned on a technicality, the TIA program sought to "revolutionize the ability of the United States to detect, classify and identify foreign terrorists" by developing data-mining and data-profiling technologies that could analyze commercial transactions and private communications. According to its Web site, which briefly featured a panoptic eye and the Latin slogan for "Knowledge is power," "Total Information Awareness of transnational threats requires keeping track of individuals and understanding how they fit into models." To this end, TIA sought to develop architectures for integrating existing databases into a "virtual centralized grand database" that would collect data from public- and private-sector sources. By analyzing financial records, educational records, travel records, and medical records, as well as criminal and other governmental records, TIA proposed to develop technologies that could create risk profiles of millions of American citizens and visitors, looking for suspicious patterns of behavior. In addition to developing biometric technologies that could pick people out of crowds and identify them from afar, the TIA program also sought to promote tools for "correlating information in the database to derive actionable intelligence," by converting speech to text, for example, or finding information in foreign languages. Although Congress refused to fund the TIA program in its current incarnation (and although it was swiftly renamed "Terrorist Information Awareness"), the data-mining and data-profiling technologies that it proposed are models for other systems that are being studied and adopted by government agencies across America and around the globe.

There is, in fact, nothing inherently good or evil about technologies of identification that seek to separate terrorists from law-abiding citizens. Nearly all of these technologies can be designed in ways that strike better or worse balances between liberty and security. Depending on these design choices, the technologies can protect liberty and security at the same time, or they can threaten liberty without bringing a corresponding increase in security. For this reason, it would be foolish to be either a technopositivist or a Luddite when evaluating proposed technological weapons in the war on terrorism. "Depending on how these technologies are designed, they can respect traditional values of liberty or not," argues Lawrence Lessig, the Stanford law professor, "and whether they do or not depends on the values that drive the designers and the institutions we build to check the design."

This chapter will explore the range of design choices presented by the new technologies of identification, and the benefits and dangers they pose. Nearly all of the new technologies can, in theory, be designed along the lines of the Blob Machine rather than the Naked Machine, in ways that protect liberty and security at the same time. But the technologists, left to their own devices, are indifferent about the balance between liberty and security; they are creatures of the market, and the market prefers to collect as much information as possible. The attitude of the technologists is well captured by the old Tom Lehrer song about the Nazi scientist who defected to America:

"Once ze rockets are up, who cares where they come down? That's not my department," says Wernher von Braun.

AS ALWAYS, ENTREPRENEURS are following the money. In January 2001, this led them to Las Vegas for the Consumer Electronics Show, the largest trade show of futuristic gadgets in North America. After 9/11, the conference organizers decided to sponsor a special exhibition hall at the Riviera Hotel for technologies that were especially well suited to homeland defense. That old familiar gold-rush feeling was in the air at the Riviera: One speaker estimated that federal spending on security technologies would grow by 30 percent a year, rising to $62 billion by 2006. In Las Vegas, several companies predicted that profiling techniques that were now used to detect credit card fraud could be used to detect potential terrorists, and soon this prediction became a reality: *The Washington Post* reported that the U.S. Department of Transportation had asked several technology companies to propose an expansion of the Computer Assisted Passenger Profiling System, or CAPPS, at airports that could analyze each passenger's living arrangements and travel and real-estate history, along with a great deal of demographic, financial, and other personal information.[3] Drawing on the same principles of mass dataveillance that were at the center of the Total Information Awareness Program, the program proposed to label travelers as "green," "yellow," or "red" security risks and to share "yellow" designations with other government and international agencies. In developing a prototype for the expanded data mining, the largest grant went to HNC Software, a risk-detection company whose software had previously been used to detect money laundering and credit card fraud. HNC uses "neural networks," a complex statistical-modeling technique that attempts to identify subtle patterns and relationships in vast amounts of unrelated data. By examining millions of data records, the company can find consistent connections that may help to predict certain patterns of behavior.

Neural-network technology has discovered that people who commit credit card fraud often fit a consistent profile—using the stolen card to buy gas at self-service stations, for example, and then using it to buy clothes at a mall. If you fit the profile of people who commit fraud by using a stolen credit card to buy gas and then clothes, you are likely to get a call from the credit card fraud detection unit. HNC also uses neural networks as a form of consumer intelligence for direct marketers. To identify potential customers for a new gourmet kitchen appliance, a neural network can be told who bought the new product and also what other products those customers bought. By identifying subtle links in buying patterns, the network can create a profile of other people who are likely to buy the new product, and these lucky consumers can then be lavished with attention from direct marketers. Data mining is said to have revealed, for example, that young fathers on late-night shopping trips often buy beer and diapers at the same time; this insight allows Wal-Mart to place the beer near the diapers.

HNC proposed to use this same neural-network technology to assign each passenger in America a "threat index" at airports based on his or her resemblance to a terrorist profile. Passengers who scored within the top 10 percent or so of the threat index could be taken aside for special questioning, along with a small percentage of people who would be flagged randomly. Joseph Sirosh, executive director of advanced technology solutions at HNC, told me that the company wanted to examine not only the passenger data that airlines maintained as part of the old Computer Assisted Passenger Profiling System—such as travel history, address, and telephone number—but also publicly available marketing data that is currently maintained by private companies. This could include living arrangements, household income, pet ownership, personal buying habits, and even lists of the books we buy and the music we listen to. In addition, HNC hoped to include personal data whose use is currently restricted by law, including records of individual credit card purchases of fertilizer or flight school lessons, for example, or international telephone calls to Afghanistan. In order for the system to obtain this data, however, the nation's privacy laws would need to be relaxed. Federal laws currently restrict the personally identifiable information that the government can demand from credit card and phone companies, except as part of a specific investigation. (The Fair Credit Reporting Act limits the cases in which a credit report can be disclosed to the government, for example; and the Computer Matching and Privacy Protection Act of 1988 forbids federal agencies from merging databases.) In response to the objections of privacy advocates, a more recent version of CAPPS, known as the Computer Assisted Passenger Pre-Screening Program, or CAPPS II, promises to examine only publicly available information.

The strongest objection to profiling and data-mining schemes that purport to increase national security is that, in their current incarnation, many seem unlikely to work. Unlike people who commit credit card fraud—a form of systematic, repetitive, and predictable behavior that fits a consistent profile identified by millions of transactions—there is no reason to believe that terrorists in the future will resemble those in the past. There were only nineteen hijackers on 9/11, and those who followed them weren't Saudi Arabians who went to flight school in Florida: they included Richard Reid, the English citizen who hid bombs in his sneakers, and who had a Jamaican father and an English mother. By trying to identify people who look like the 9/11 hijackers, the profiling scheme is looking for a needle in a haystack, but the color and the shape of the needle keep changing. "Some terrorism experts are skeptical about terrorist profiling," according to a 1999 report prepared by the Library of Congress for U.S. intelligence agencies. "There seems to be general agreement among psychologists that there is no particular psychological attribute that can be used to describe the terrorist or any 'personality' that is distinctive of terrorists."[4] For this reason, the U.S. Secret Service, which once looked for people who fit profiles of stereotypes of presidential assassins, has abandoned its personality profiles and now looks for patterns of motive or behavior.[5]

Moreover, because the sample of known terrorists is so small, attempts to identify suspects with electronic profiles are bound to produce a high number of "false positives"—that is, passengers whom the system wrongly identifies as possible terrorists—and the costs of the system are likely to outweigh its benefits. To illustrate why data-profiling systems are ineffective in looking for needles in haystacks, Christopher Guzelian and Mariano-Florentino Cuéllar of Stanford Law School note that at one point, doctors used to recommend monitoring large numbers of people for signs of latent diseases such as diabetes or ovarian, lung, and skin cancers. But because of the inaccuracy of profiling systems in identifying symptoms that occur very rarely in the population at large, the medical establishment concluded that the benefits of monitoring were outweighed by the costs, which include not only false positives (people wrongly identified as being sick) but also false negatives (people wrongly identified as being healthy).[6] Guzelian and Cuéllar give the example of a monitoring system that is searching for a disease that occurs in 20 out of every 10,000 people. Assume that the accuracy of the profiling system is 90 percent. Of the 20 people who have the disease, 18 (that's 90 percent of 20) will test positive and be correctly identified. Two of the 20 people with the disease will be missed by the system and falsely test negative. That leaves 9,980 people who don't have the disease.

Of this group, the number who correctly test negative will be 8,982 (90 percent of 9,980). In other words, 998 people without the disease will wrongly test positive, and all of them will have to be subject to intrusive follow-up tests with extensive risks. A false-positive rate like this is generally considered too high to be justified.

In the case of terrorism, of course, the prevalence of potential terrorists in the population as a whole is unknown. But imagine a profiling system that was set up to identify the nineteen hijackers of 9/11. Searching for nineteen individuals in a population of 300 million would yield exponentially more false positives: Even assuming the profiling system were 99 percent accurate, because of the low prevalence rate, 3,000,000 (that's 0.01×300 million) of those identified as potential terrorists by the system would be wrongly accused. Such a system would bring the nation's airports to a halt. In other words, only 0.000363 percent of the people who tested positive in a nearly perfect system actually would be positive—a success rate so low that the system would have to be stopping a nuclear bomb on the benefits side and imposing little more than a pat-down on the costs side to be justified. But in fact, of course, no data-mining system has proved to be 99 percent accurate in predicting terrorist behavior, because the new attacks so rarely resemble the previous ones. A system with only 1 percent accuracy would falsely accuse nearly all innocent travelers of being terrorists and correctly identify only a fraction of terrorists while missing nearly all of the real terrorists. No rational evaluation of costs and benefits would support the adoption of such a hopeless system as an effective tool for national security. For this reason, efforts to use dataveillance as a way of predicting terrorist behavior in the population at large, rather than investigating individuals who have been identified as terrorists by other means, seems empirically dubious.

An expanded CAPPS profile might also be easy for terrorists to defeat. Even if the profile itself is kept secret, terrorist cells could recruit sympathizers who tend not to set off alarm bells and encourage them to go through security to see whether or not they have been tagged by the system for a special search. Individuals who established their lack of suspiciousness could then return to the airport on destructive missions in the future. Mohammad Atta himself tested the CAPPS system in precisely this way: He practiced his attack in the weeks before 9/11 by boarding the same flights he later intended to hijack to ensure that he didn't set off any electronic alarms. This is why targeted searches based on human intelligence are likely to be more effective at catching terrorists than computer algorithms.[7]

The technologists are undaunted by practical questions about whether it makes sense to profile terrorists the way they profile e-business consumers. Instead, they are driven by the market above all. In the glory days of the late 1990s, Silicon Valley was consumed by the search for the "killer app," the software application that was so cool and effective that everyone had to buy it. After 9/11, the consensus in the valley is that the "killer app" for national security will allow government agencies to access and share information about Americans that is currently stored in different databases—from our chat-room gossip to our shopping history to our parking tickets, and perhaps even to our payment history for child-support checks.

"Today, every federal intelligence and law-enforcement agency and all manner of state and local bodies maintain their own separate databases on suspected criminals," Larry Ellison, the founder and CEO of Oracle Corporation, wrote in *The Wall Street Journal* a month after 9/11. "Do we need more databases? No, just the opposite. The biggest problem today is that we have too many. The single thing we could do to make life tougher for terrorists would be to ensure that all the information in myriad government databases was integrated into a single national file."[8] Oracle, as it happens, is the world's largest database manufacturer, and Ellison offered to donate the software for a single national database to the United States government free of charge. (The company, Ellison added, would charge for upgrades and maintenance.) Oracle's office in Reston, Virginia, is near the headquarters of the CIA, which is appropriate enough: When Larry Ellison founded the company twenty-five years ago, his first client was the CIA, to whom he sold a program called Oracle, the world's first commercially available "relational" database. At that time, information in computer databases was stored in unrelated files: A company like Ford, for example, could keep one file of its employees and another file of its departments, but it had no easy way of relating the two files. Ellison saw the commercial potential of the relational database and began marketing it in 1979. By the height of the dot-com boom in 2000, Ellison's net worth had soared to $80 billion, making him (briefly) the richest person in the world.

When I visited Oracle, the security guard in the lobby gave me a high-tech ID badge that could track where I was in the building at all times. I was ushered upstairs to a bright conference room where seven people were sitting around a huge oval table. One of them, David Carey, turned out to be the former number three man at the CIA; he had just retired as executive director after thirty-two years with the agency. Carey joined Oracle to head its new Information Assurance Center, which was founded in November 2001, to design homeland-security and disaster-recovery solutions and market them to the federal government. Like his colleagues, Carey was in an expansive mood. He said that the United States government accounted for 23 percent of Oracle's multibillion-dollar licensing revenue last year and that he expected the federal side of the business to improve after 9/11. "How do you say this without sounding callous?" he asked. "In some ways, 9/11 made business a bit easier. Previous to 9/11, you pretty much had to hype the threat and the problem." Carey said that the summer before the attacks, leaders in the public and private sectors wouldn't sit still for a briefing. Then his face brightened. "Now they clamor for it!"

I asked to see an example of Oracle's new homeland-security technology, and I was ushered into a demonstration hall outside the conference room that looked like something out of *The Matrix*. "I'll give you an overview of LEADERS," said Brian Jones, then the head of Oracle's health-care consulting unit. "It stands for Lightweight Epidemiology Advanced Detection and Emergency Response System." By collecting health-care information from hospital emergency rooms across the country, LEADERS is designed to monitor outbreaks of suspicious diseases and provide early warnings for biological attacks. At 9:20 A.M. on 9/11, Jones had received a phone call from the Centers for Disease Control and Prevention in Atlanta, which feared that the attack on the Twin Towers might be followed by a bioterrorism attack. Working for ten straight hours, Jones put into his computer the address of every hospital in New York State, to detect unusual disease outbreaks, like smallpox. "Every hospital was capable of submitting data to a repository," he explained. "The Centers for Disease Control's experts could sit back in Atlanta and pull up a map just like I'm showing you here." Jones punched a key, and a digital map of New York City appeared on the screen. Using a combination of 7,500 digital photographs and architectural plans of more than 6,000 miles of underground pipes, Oracle has created a detailed map of every building, sewer and water line, and curb in the city. By the evening of 9/11, Jones was ready to monitor every emergency-room bed in the state. Working with the federal government, Oracle hopes to apply the same surveillance system to hospitals throughout the country. The system would allow hospitals to report incidents of suspicious diseases like anthrax, smallpox, and Ebola to a central database. The program could then send out e-mail or voice-mail alerts to law enforcement officials if it detected suspicious patterns of diseases anywhere in the country. Steve Cooperman, Oracle's director of homeland security, said, "We're going to build a bioterrorism shield, so eventually everyone is going to have to participate—every hospital, every clinic, every lab."

The prospect of every hospital in America reporting their patients' medical conditions to a central Oracle database might cause some people alarm. But Oracle insists that the information can be stored in ways that can't be linked to individual patients, making possible syndromic surveillance that identifies suspicious trends without identifying individuals in ways that might violate privacy. And if the system operates as Oracle says it will, syndromic surveillance promises genuine benefits with a low cost to privacy. It is a model for other forms of syndromic surveillance that have used Oracle technology with impressive results. Working with the city of Chicago, for example, Oracle has created an integrated criminal database and then applied data-mining technologies to predict where the next crime waves are likely to occur. For example, if the profiling software finds that gun-related gang fights tend to occur in certain neighborhoods, on days with certain weather patterns and sporting events, the police can send extra forces to the neighborhood on the evening of a big game. The trends tend to be reliable, and because the profiling focuses on patterns of group activity rather than on particular individuals, it's hard to object that anyone's privacy has been invaded.

A far greater potential for invasions of privacy is raised by Larry Ellison's proposal to centralize all of the separate criminal databases run by federal and state authorities into a single national database, which would link personal data to individuals in identifiable ways. "We think of it as a triangle," said Tim Hoechst, a senior vice president for technology at Oracle, holding up a Dorito. "At one corner is privacy, at one corner is assurance of security—how safe is the data—and at another corner is usability. It's all a matter of trade-offs. What we focus on is making the Dorito here, and putting you in any corner that you feel comfortable with."

But as databases are consolidated, who should decide the proper balance between liberty and security, privacy and access? How would Oracle avoid a situation in which someone could be kept off a plane because he or she had skipped jury duty or had an overdue parking ticket? "You'll notice that we all became suspiciously quiet when we started talking about policy questions," Hoechst replied after a long pause. "At Oracle, we leave that to our customers to decide. We become a little stymied when we start talking about the 'should-we's' and the 'whys' and the 'hows,' because it's not our expertise."

"I expect that if you ask Larry Ellison the question, he'd give you a much better answer," one of Hoechst's associates chimed in. Hoechst agreed. "My experience with him is that he knows an extraordinary amount about a lot of things. Every time I think I know something, he knows much more. He's read more books on it."

So I set off for Silicon Valley to meet Larry Ellison. The Oracle campus near the San Francisco airport is known as the Emerald City, for its artificial lakes and silo-shaped towers of glass and silver. Ellison's private palace, however, is a $30 million mansion in nearby Atherton, modeled on the Katsura Imperial Villa in Kyoto. I was checked in there by two bodyguards with dark shirts and dark tans and escorted into the house to wait. The living room was large and airy, with lots of blond wood and shoji screens. It overlooked a beautiful Japanese garden, where ducks swam and waterfalls shimmered. Ellison appeared a few minutes later from behind one of the screens, wearing a pressed charcoal suit over a black turtleneck. He appeared fit and tanned, with piercing hazel eyes and a trimmed beard slightly flecked with gray. He suggested that we talk in the garden, but the loud whine of a neighbor's mulcher made this impossible. (In Silicon Valley, even $30 million doesn't buy you quiet.) Defeated by the noise, we retreated to the dining room, with its high-backed black lacquer chairs and black lacquer table.

Ellison is not a shy or enigmatic billionaire. He is entertainingly indiscreet—he answered every question with a torrent of confident opinions. "The Oracle database is used to keep track of basically everything," he said. "The information about your banks, your checking balance, your savings balance, is stored in an Oracle database. Your airline reservation is stored in an Oracle database. What books you bought on Amazon is stored in an Oracle database. Your profile on Yahoo! is stored in an Oracle database." Much of the information in these separate commercial databases is also centralized in large databases maintained by credit card companies like TRW to detect fraud and to decide whether customers should get credit at the mall. When it comes to government data, by contrast, there are hundreds of separate, disconnected databases. "The huge problem is the fragmented data," Ellison said. "We knew Mohammad Atta was wanted. It's just that we didn't check the right database when he came into the country." Ellison wants to consolidate the hundreds of separate state and federal databases into a single Oracle database, using the centralized credit card databases as a model. "We already have this large centralized database to keep track of where you work, how much you earn, where your kids go to school, were you late on your last mortgage payment, when's the last time you got a raise," he said. "Well, my God, there are hundreds of places we have to look to see if you're a security risk." He dismissed the risks of privacy violations: "I really don't understand. Central databases already exist. Privacy is already gone."

As Ellison spoke, it occurred to me that he was proposing to reconstruct America's national security strategy along the lines of Oracle's business model. When Oracle moved its business to the Internet in 1995, Ellison complained that its customer information was scattered across hundreds of separate databases, which meant that the German office couldn't share information about customers with the French office. By consolidating 130 separate databases into a single database on the Internet, Ellison said, Oracle saved $1 billion a year and found it easier to track, monitor, and discriminate among its customers. This was what Ellison now wanted to do for America.

I asked if there would be any controls on access to the database. For example, would Ellison want people to be kept off a plane because they were late on their alimony payments? "Oh, no, I don't think we would keep anyone off on alimony payments," Ellison said. "But if the system designed to catch terrorists also catches mere bank robbers and deadbeat dads, that's okay. I think that's a good thing. I don't think it's a bad thing."

There are, at the moment, legal restrictions prohibiting the sharing of data by government agencies. The most important restriction was passed in 1974, to prevent President Nixon from ordering dragnet surveillance of Vietnam protesters and searching for their youthful marijuana arrests. I asked Ellison whether these legal restrictions should be relaxed. "Oh, absolutely," he said. "I mean absolutely. The prohibitions are absurd. It's this fear of an all-too-powerful government rising up and snatching away our liberties." Since 9/11, Ellison argued, those qualms no longer made any sense: "It's our lives that are at risk, not our liberties," he said.

Ellison proposes to link the central government database to a system of digital identification cards that would be optional for citizens but mandatory for aliens. He wants each cardholder to provide a thumbprint or an iris scan that would be stored in the central database. I noted that a national fingerprint database was probably the most invasive of all possible designs for an identification system, because it would allow the government to dust for fingerprints in a nightclub or a protest scene and identify everyone who was there. I asked Ellison why the government couldn't minimize these privacy concerns by storing the fingerprint on the ID card. Ellison dismissed the suggestion. "Everyone's got this amorphous idea that the government will somehow misuse this," he said, "but no one has given me a substantive example of what will happen that's bad." I tried again. What about the centralized storage of health information, as Oracle was proposing to do with LEADERS? Would Ellison want government officials to have access to personally identifiable genetic information? "I feel like Alice has fallen through the looking glass," Ellison said. His voice rose; he was starting to get a little testy. "Does this other database bother you here? We can't touch that database because I won't be able to use my credit card. Like, I won't be able to go to the mall!" He took on the voice of Sean Penn in *Fast Times at Ridgemont High*. "Like, that's really disturbing. Like, don't mess with my mall experience. Okay, so people have to die over here without this, but that's not going to affect my experience going to the mall." He exhaled, and in his regular billionaire voice asked, "I mean, what the hell is going on?"

Ellison said he was late for an appointment at Intel and started to make motions to leave. I tried one more question. Were there no differences between Oracle and the United States government, I asked, that should make us hesitate before centralizing all of our national databases using Oracle as a model? "From the information-science standpoint, there's no difference at all," he replied. "These central databases are cheaper and better and they solve all these problems. We can manage credit risks that way. We should be managing security risks in exactly the same way."

It's not surprising, of course, that Larry Ellison sincerely believes that what's good for Oracle is good for America. But there are, in fact, differences between an e-business and the American government, differences that should make us hesitate before reconstructing America along the business model of the Oracle Corporation. "Once the business data have been centralized and integrated, the value of the database is greater than the sum of the preexisting—scattered—parts. (This is Ellison's Law)," the Oracle manifesto, *E-Business or Out of Business,* announces reverentially. But the U.S. Constitution insists that in the design of structures of government, centralized power must be checked to protect fundamental constitutional values. (This is America's law.) Therefore, a database that respected constitutional values would contain structural checks and balances, to ensure that the state tracked its citizens less intrusively than an e-business tracked its customers.

Ellison has proposed the most efficient and most invasive card possible, which could allow the government to dust for fingerprints at a protest scene, plug the fingerprints into a centralized fingerprint database, and identify against their will everyone who was at the protest scene. (This is called "one-to-many" identification.) Any architecture of identity that stores a fingerprint in a central database makes it easy for the government to track a great deal of personal information—including what we have bought and where we have been. For example, a welfare recipient who leaves fingerprints at a nightclub that later becomes a crime scene could be identified if the police plugged the print into a fingerprint database maintained for all welfare recipients. The police could then show up at his or her door. Even if laws restricted the use of the fingerprint database, the laws could be changed, or the database could be hacked.[9]

IF ELLISON'S CARD is the equivalent of the Naked Machine, it's possible to design an ID card that looks more like the Blob Machine, protecting privacy and security at the same time. The Blob version of the privacy card would be limited to "one-to-one" verification rather than "one-to-many" identification, confirming that a particular person is who he or she claims to be without allowing the government to pick him or her out of a crowd. George Tomko, the husband of Ann Cavoukian, who is the privacy commissioner of Ontario, Canada, has designed a verification system based on biometric encryption that provides complete security and complete privacy. In 1990, Tomko founded an innovative company that makes it possible to lock packets of data in encrypted files, using your fingerprint as a private key. "Let's say there's a parcel of information that's required to cross a border," Tomko told me. "You take that parcel of information and encrypt it with your fingerprint. . . . When you go to the border, they download your file, you slide your finger, and if you decrypt your file correctly, then you are who you say you are. So now you have absolute privacy with absolute security." Assuming (and this is a big assumption) that the fingerprints aren't stored anywhere, individuals retain complete control over how much information about themselves to reveal.

Tomko's technology could also be used to design a profiling

system that protects privacy and security at the same time. He notes that a database with the health information of millions of citizens could be anonymized by separating the information itself from the identity of particular individuals. Scientists could study trends in genetic or infectious diseases without being able to link the information to particular individuals without their consent. A computer pointer, encrypted by a fingerprint, would provide the link between an individual's identity and his or her health data, and individuals would be free to refuse to unlock the pointer unless ordered by a court. "Biometric encryption," Tomko concludes hopefully, "provides the technological basis for informational self-determination."[10]

Citizens who were confident that the government couldn't identify them personally unless they presented an extremely high risk of posing a terrorist threat might be more willing to give the government access to information that is currently restricted by law. Researchers have studied data-mining systems that protect privacy by randomizing personal data, allowing accurate generalizations about patterns of behavior without giving officials access to individual data records. For example, instead of being identified as a twenty-one-year-old man, a citizen could be identified as someone between the ages of twenty and twenty-five. The randomization methods allow for predictions (about the buying habits of Generation Xers, for example) that tend to be as accurate as the unrandomized data.

In theory, profiling systems at airports could also be constructed in ways that separate the anonymized data from identifiable individuals, allowing the government to reconstitute the link between an individual and the data only when the system has developed a very high degree of suspicion that the individual poses a serious threat.[11] "I think that the general form of the correct solution is traceable but not identifiable data," says Lawrence Lessig. "In traceable but not identifiable data, you need structures to prevent improper tracing and improper access to the data, and that means you need a regime of checks and balances to regulate the tracing." As a model, he gives the example of the clipper chip, a technology that would have given the government backdoor access to all encrypted data. Encryption is a technology that makes data (nearly) impossible to read without a key, and the clipper chip would have given the government a special key that enabled it (but no one else) to decrypt data without the sender's consent. When attempts to persuade industry to adopt the clipper chip by subsidizing it failed, the government proposed to require the authors of encryption code to build a back door through which the government could gain access. "We had none of the right intuitions about the clipper chip," says Lessig. "The government wanted to have the key held by a particular government agency, but the agency was reportable to the president in the same way the FBI was reportable to Nixon. A better solution would have been to split the key: Put half in the executive branch and half in the judicial branch and say that if the executive wants access to the key, the judicial branch has to say it's okay to turn over. That's a classically Madisonian form of checks and balances, to make sure the thing doesn't get deployed improperly."

Mass dataveillance might, in theory, be regulated by similar legal and technological checks and balances, to ensure that data is traceable but not immediately identifiable. The Defense Advanced Research Projects Agency, or DARPA, which brought us the Total Information Awareness program, has also been studying technologies of "selective revelation," which minimize personally identifiable information while allowing data mining and analysis on a grand scale. "The idea of selective revelation is that initially we reveal information to the analyst only in sanitized form, that is, in terms of statistics and categories that do not reveal (directly or indirectly) anyone's private information," says a DARPA report called *Security with Privacy*. "If the analyst sees reason for concern he or she can follow up by seeking permission to get more precise information. This permission would be granted if the initial information provides sufficient cause to allow the revelation of more information, under appropriate legal and policy guidelines."[12] The report gives the example of an analyst who asks whether any individual has recently bought suspicious quantities of chemicals and rented a large truck. The algorithm replies yes or no, without revealing the identity of any particular individual, and the analyst could then ask a judge for permission to learn the individual's name. Selective-revelation technologies build on recent work that allows information to be searched in databases without revealing the queries or the results to the databases themselves. This technology would allow government agencies to search data from private data warehouses such as Acxiom without revealing the nature of the searches to Acxiom. But without careful oversight of these secret searches—including audit trails that are reviewed by independent agencies—it's easy to imagine opportunities for abuse.

The DARPA Information Awareness Office has a project called Genisys that is exploring ways of conducting general data searches where the data are traceable but not easily identifiable—in other words, generally anonymous unless officials receive permission to link the data with a particular individual. According to the program director, Genisys could protect privacy by separating identifying information from personal transactions, only re-creating the association when there is evidence and legal authority to do so. This might allow, for example, the Centers for Disease Control and Prevention to have access to medical information while other groups do not. The Genisys staff also plans to develop information-privacy filters to keep information that is not relevant out of the repository—encouraging the government to adopt laws that limit the types of data that can be recorded about specific people or transactions. Finally, Genisys plans to use software agents to mine the information in the repository to expunge information that is unrelated to terrorism.[13]

These are promising first steps toward the creation of an architecture of surveillance that might, in theory, protect liberty and security by imposing controls on how data is used, but it's clear that privacy can't be protected by technology alone. For the system to work, Congress would have to create a series of oversight mechanisms to ensure that the system is focusing on potential terrorists rather than on innocent citizens. Congress could also create a special oversight court with the authority to decide when identifying data obtained during mass dataveillance may be connected to transactional information. After intelligence analysts have identified a series of transactions that they believe might be evidence of a terrorist plan, they could petition the special court for authorization to identify the individuals concerned. In considering whether to grant the request, Congress could direct the court to satisfy itself that the crime for which evidence has been presented is a serious threat of force or violence, and that the evidence suggests a link between the suspects and organized terrorists. If the court granted the order, the analysts could link the identifying information with the transaction data, and they could contact federal, state, and local law enforcement officials to inform them of the threat. In addition to creating this oversight body and determining legal standards to guide its operation, Congress might also create standards for federal and citizen oversight, along with penalties for abuse; a dispute resolution process that would give citizens recourse when their data are incorrect or misused; and a series of fair information practices that would give citizens the right to know what personal information the government has collected, and to correct any inaccuracies.

Merely to describe the complexity of these regulations, however, is to raise legitimate questions about whether Congress and the courts are up to the collaborative effort of designing and adopting them. It's hard to conceive of the complicated convergence of technological, legislative, and judicial pressures that would have to work together to bring the privacy-protective profiling scheme into being. Instead, politicians and technologists have an incentive to put all the weight on the side of security, rather than privacy, and, as we will see in chapter 4, neither the courts nor Congress is in the habit of insisting on a more reasonable balance. For this reason, Lessig has become pessimistic that Silicon Valley, left to its own devices, will get the balance right. "The reality is that all the market power is going to be on the side of delivering the security, and there's no strong claim on the other side for delivering the privacy," he says. "There's no court that will stand up and push the demand for heightened review for privacy, and there's no politician.

And then you have Larry Ellison types riding in with the glow of the market."

The search for technological solutions to our new security challenges is part of a deeply American urge for perfect fairness and perfect security, extended equally and automatically to all. In our eagerness to avoid the specter of human discrimination in any form, we prefer to turn surveillance over to the purportedly objective machines. But there are dangers in putting too much faith in technologies of identification, which may lead us to underestimate the human intelligence and discretionary judgments that have proved to be the most effective way of identifying terrorists in the past. The most important intelligence breakthroughs before and after 9/11 have been the result of close scrutiny and investigation by human beings rather than of profiles produced by machines. Ahmed Ressam, the terrorist who planned to blow up the L.A. airport on New Year's Eve, 1999, was caught at the Canadian border not because he fit a computer profile or was flagged by a database (he was using an alias that defeated the profile), but because a border guard thought that he looked nervous. In the same way, as we saw in chapter 1, the ten-year-old murderers of Jamie Bulger, the two-year-old British boy, were identified not because of CCTV cameras but because they boasted to their friends.

Bruce Schneier, the author of *Applied Cryptography* and an authority in the field of computer security, argues that technological cure-alls sometimes make us less safe when they fail on a large scale. The centralized consumer databases that companies use to identify customers became magnets for criminals and caused identity theft to triple between 1995 and 2000, he argues. Centralized federal databases designed to profile terrorists would be similarly attractive to hackers and thieves. Schneier insists that profiling and screening systems that depend on vast amounts of secret data are inherently vulnerable because they can be compromised once the profiles are known. Biometric ID cards protected with encrypted fingerprints are especially dangerous, because if your thumbprint is stolen, your entire identity becomes an open book. Instead of focusing on technological fixes to problems that have little to do with terrorism (all of the 9/11 terrorists came into the country with valid visas and had photo IDs that correctly identified them by name), Schneier prefers low-tech measures that rely on humans with dispersed responsibilities: reinforced cockpit doors, encouraging passengers to fight back against hijackers, and human guards at secure checkpoints. "The trick is to remember that technology can't save you," Schneier told *The Atlantic Monthly.* "The Club at best makes burglars steal the car next to you. For real safety we park on nice streets where people notice if somebody smashes the window. . . . People are the essential security element."[14]

Americans, by contrast, are enamored with technology, and the American yearning for silver bullets after 9/11 calls to mind the technological yearning of many liberals and progressives in the first half of the twentieth century. Disillusioned by what they saw as the excesses of popular opinion during and after World War I—expressed in the Red Scare, the Prohibition Amendment, and the Scopes Trial—progressives, as Christopher Lasch has noted, turned to technology instead. "The characteristic trait of liberals nowadays," argued Matthew Josephson in 1930, "is their disappointment at finding that the people care little for liberty." Josephson insisted that liberals should "resist the majority, the vox populi, the great crowd" as well as reactionaries who sought a "return to ancient systems of authority, discipline, culture." The best hope, Josephson concluded, consisted in an orderly transition to what John Dewey and Charles Beard had called a "technological-rationalist society" despite the fact that it promised a "more valid equality" that would mean the "inevitable sacrifice" of individual liberties.[15]

The most technologically optimistic progressives urged the state to embrace purportedly scientific techniques such as eugenics, or the science of better breeding. Far from threatening liberal values, these progressives believed that compulsory sterilization and immigration restrictions were technologies of control that would protect Americans from "race suicide" and the threat posed by immigrants and aliens in their midst. The progressives had faith in the ability of enlightened experts such as themselves to design and regulate the technologies of social control and to deploy them for good rather than evil. In their enthusiasm for technologies of identification and classification, some of the technopositivists of today also have too much confidence in the power of rational experts to design technologies that will protect liberal values without unplanned side effects.

Just as the science of biometrics has its roots in the work of Francis Galton, a founder of the eugenics movement, many of the other architectures of identification and profiling today are technologies of hierarchy masquerading as technologies of equality. Rather than allowing human beings to engage in crude forms of racial profiling, which might victimize a visible group of Americans, we prefer to extend systems of profiling to all Americans. But instead of serving the values of civic equality, the purportedly egalitarian profiling technologies end up classifying and ranking all Americans with more ruthless precision than any human being could impose. And instead of eliminating the evils of stereotyping and discrimination, the technologies of classification extend them across American society as a whole. There are, of course, important differences between profiling based on immutable characteristics, such as race or national origin, and profiling based on past behavior; and for this reason the former is more objectionable than the latter. But in their willingness to make judgments about individuals based on crude generalizations about widely shared attributes, both forms of profiling run the risk of judging individuals out of context and unfairly tarring them on the basis of characteristics they can no longer control.

The government's eagerness to rank American citizens by using the technologies that were designed to rank American consumers confuses the values of the market with the values of a constitutional democracy. The American government shouldn't be in the business of ranking its citizens based on the government's estimation of the citizens' trustworthiness. Under our Constitution, the government is supposed to win the trust of its citizens, not the other way around. In this sense, the architectures of identification, as currently designed, misunderstand the difference between a company's relationship with its customers and a state's relationship with its citizens. "A single integrated record-set for each customer confers prodigious advantages on the corporation that possesses it," declares the Oracle manifesto, *E-Business or Out of Business*. "It empowers every employee of the corporation to relate to the customer in terms consistent with the corporate view of the customer reality. . . . Customers are *not* interchangeable."[16]

America, unlike an e-business, isn't supposed to relate to citizens in terms consistent with the government view of the citizen's reality. In America, individuals are supposed to be free to define and redefine their own reality, free from government efforts to predict their behavior in the future based on their behavior in the past. In the eyes of the law, individuals are indeed interchangeable and equal, and they are entitled not to be profiled and classified based on secret searches of personal information that the government refuses to disclose.

The entrepreneurs of Silicon Valley like to think of themselves as antigovernment libertarians, and the business nostrums of the era before the dot-com crash assumed that the Internet would lead inevitably to the end of hierarchy and centralized authority and the flourishing of individual creativity. When the e-business technologies of tracking, classifying, profiling, and monitoring were used to identify the preferences of American consumers and to mirror back to each of us a market-segmented version of ourselves, Silicon Valley could argue that it was serving the cause of freedom and individual choice. But when the same software applications are used by the government to track, classify, profile, and monitor American citizens, they become not technologies of liberty but technologies of state surveillance and discrimination. Far from leading inevitably to the end of centralized authority, the age of the Internet turns out to include powerful economic and political forces that are determined to centralize as much information about individuals as possible. "The commonest solutions to the problem of mass surveillance in large-scale societies lie in the use of documentation," wrote the sociologist James Rule in the 1970s. "The formal rendering of information about people comes to take the place of informal mechanisms of surveillance found in small-scale settings. The crucial function of such documentation is to link people to their pasts, and thereby to provide the surveillance necessary for the exercise of social control."[17]

There is something especially presumptuous about Silicon Valley's conceit that technology can solve the "Tower of Babel problem," and that machines can classify, analyze, and understand all of the fragmented data in the world. After all, it was a misplaced faith in the limitless power of technology that created the Tower of Babel in the first place. In the beginning, according to Genesis 11, all of the people of the earth lived in one place and spoke one language. To celebrate their unity and to make a name for themselves, they decided to build a city with a tower that would reach all the way to heaven. God was affronted by this act of technological hubris, which reflected the mistaken belief that architecture alone could create proximity to the all-seeing divine. To put the people in their place, God scattered them across the earth, making it impossible for them to understand one another's speech. The Tower of Babel, in other words, is a monument to the technological overconfidence that results when human beings perceive themselves to be united, transparent, and equal to God. This creates the mistaken belief, as Genesis puts it, that "nothing that they propose to do will now be impossible for them."

Now Silicon Valley and Washington are trying to reconstruct the global village that God dispersed, once again yearning to centralize all the world's data into one place and to translate it into a common language. This is an act of hubris that should make even an oracle pause. "In twenty years, do you think the global database is going to exist, and will it be run by Oracle?" I asked Larry Ellison. "I do think it will exist and I think it is going to be an Oracle database," he said. "And we're going to track everything."

CHAPTER FOUR

The Path of the Law

"WAR IS THE HEALTH OF THE STATE," RANDOLPH Bourne wrote sardonically during World War I. "It automatically sets in motion throughout society those irresistible forces for uniformity, for passionate cooperation with the Government in coercing into obedience the minority groups and individuals which lack the larger herd sense."[1] A hunchback, a socialist, and a critic for *The New Republic,* Bourne described how during the Great War, public opinion had become a solid and oppressive block. "Minority opinion, which in times of peace was only irritating . . . , becomes, with the outbreak of war, a cause for outlawry. Criticism of the State, objections to war, luke-warm opinions concerning the necessity or the beauty of conscription, are made subject to ferocious penalties, far exceeding in severity those affixed to actual pragmatic crimes."[2] All this, Bourne wrote, was the inevitable consequence of the herd instinct of the crowd when it feels that its security has been attacked. "In your reaction to an imagined attack on your country or an insult to its government," he declared, "you draw closer to the herd for protection, you conform in word and deed, and you insist vehemently that everybody else shall think, speak and act together."[3]

After 9/11, many civil libertarians predicted similar infringements of civil liberties;[4] but, in the end, our worst fears did not come to pass. In a more individualistic and egalitarian age, the herd instinct expresses itself in demands for personal security rather than patriotic conformity. As a result, none of the legal excesses that followed 9/11 could compare to those that followed World War I—from the deportation of suspected anarchists to the imprisonment of antiwar socialists. The flag-waving president and his apocalyptic attorney general, like their predecessors in wartime, pressed for sweeping increases in executive authority, based on the novel claim that the president had the unilateral power to detain and investigate American citizens and aliens without oversight from Congress or the courts. But the courts and Congress, unlike their predecessors in wartime, rejected some of the president's most extreme claims. Federal judges insisted on the importance of judicial oversight of some of the president's powers of detention and deportation. And in the debates over the USA Patriot Act and the creation of a Department of Homeland Security, libertarians on the right joined with civil libertarians on the left in persuading Congress to repudiate several of the administration's most draconian proposals for expanded surveillance authority, including the Total Information Awareness data-mining project, at least for the moment. In this sense, the most reliable protector of American liberty turned out to be something so basic that we often take it for granted: the checks and balances provided by the separation of powers in the Constitution.

But although libertarians in the courts and U.S. Congress resisted some of the executive's most sweeping demands, they were less successful in proposing more balanced alternatives. The great challenge presented by the expansion of surveillance powers after 9/11 is the need for legal regulations that require the government to protect liberty as well as security, ensuring that the most invasive forms of surveillance are targeted on the most serious crimes. There are, as I will explore in the epilogue, a number of ways of trying to design these regulations, which could be imposed by judges or legislators. In this chapter, I will argue that Congress is better equipped than the courts to design regulations that protect liberty, privacy, and security at the same time. This conclusion may seem counterintuitive: Americans sometimes lionize their judges as heroic checks on the passions of the crowd and denigrate their representatives as a group of self-interested political opportunists. But the comparative performances of the courts and Congress after 9/11 point to a very different conclusion: Courts were (properly) reluctant to second-guess popular conceptions of how much privacy citizens should reasonably expect. By contrast, Congress proved better equipped to strike pragmatic compromises about the balance between liberty and security.

Let's begin with Congress, where the most ardent defenders of liberty and privacy after 9/11 represented a vocal but distinctively American libertarian minority. After 9/11, an unusual alliance emerged between libertarian and religious conservatives, who remembered the FBI's attacks on antigovernment conservatives at Ruby Ridge and Waco during the Clinton era, and civil libertarians on the left, who remembered the FBI's surveillance of Vietnam protesters during the Nixon era. As Congress debated the administration's proposal to create a new Department of Homeland Security, a schism developed between John Ashcroft and his allies on the religious right. Paul Weyrich, the president of the Free Congress Foundation, which had been a leading supporter of Ashcroft's nomination as attorney general, told *The New York Times* that the enthusiasm for Ashcroft among grassroots religious conservatives was waning. "There is suddenly a great concern that what . . . was passed in the wake of 9/11 were things that had little to do with catching terrorists but a lot to do with increasing the strength of government to infiltrate and spy on conservative organizations,"[5] Weyrich said. In Congress, libertarian conservatives were equally disenchanted with Bush and Ashcroft's demand for unilateral expansions of executive authority. "The attorney general doesn't seem to be making any effort to contain the lust for power that these people in the Department of Justice have," I was told by Dick Armey, the retiring House majority leader. "The Justice Department in the U.S. today, more than any federal agency, seems to be running amok and out of control." Representative Bob Barr of Georgia, the former Clinton impeachment manager, was equally distressed. "What has been especially troubling in the wake of the enactment of the Patriot Act," he told me, "is that the administration has been resisting any effort to provide information to the judiciary committee detailing how its work is being implemented."

If civil libertarians had to pick the members of Congress most responsible for the defense of liberty since 9/11, Armey and Barr, along with a group of Democratic allies, such as Patrick Leahy of Vermont and Russell Feingold of Wisconsin, would be at the top of the list. Their principled opposition to the expansion of federal authority helped to ensure that the version of the USA Patriot Act that Bush signed was less draconian than the initial draft he and Ashcroft had proposed. Because of Armey's efforts, half of the new surveillance powers in the Patriot Act will expire in four years, and the administration must report to Congress about its implementation. Similarly, the law creating a new Department of Homeland Security repudiated a national ID card,[6] and it rejected Ashcroft's proposed Terrorism Information and Prevention System, or TIPS, which would have encouraged deliverymen to spy on their customers and neighbors, reporting on suspicious activities. Most important of all, Congress created oversight mechanisms for the so-called Carnivore e-mail searching program, which allows the government to scan millions of innocent e-mails while searching for evidence of guilt. And a bipartisan majority in Congress was successfully mobilized to bar funding of the data-mining project known as Total Information Awareness, unless the Defense Department submitted a report to Congress on its effectiveness and impact on civil liberties, or unless the president told Congress that the bar would endanger national security. "The Total Information Awareness programs should not be used to develop technologies for use in conducting intelligence activities or law enforcement activities against United States persons without appropriate consultation with Congress or without clear adherence to principle to protect civil liberty and privacy," Congress declared in a unanimous statement.[7]

How was a libertarian, bipartisan movement mobilized in Congress to resist executive excesses after 9/11? At the beginning of the twenty-first century, the defenders of big government include the neoconservative unilateralists and Republican moralists on the right and mainstream Democrats on the left, while its conservative critics are the libertarian wing, represented by Armey and Barr and thinkers associated with the Cato Institute; evangelical Christians who are concerned about One World Government; and the America Firsters, who oppose federal power because of their nativist determination to preserve traditional jobs and family values at the local level. John Ashcroft tried unsuccessfully to straddle these warring factions in the Republican Party: He was an evangelical from Missouri who had expressed some reservations about federal power as a senator but abandoned those scruples when he moved from criticizing the Justice Department to running it. "Now, more than ever, we must protect citizens' privacy from the excesses of an arrogant, overly powerful government," Ashcroft said in opposing the Clinton administration's policies about encryption on the Internet in 1998. "Law enforcement is using advances in digital technology as an excuse to insist on intrusions into privacy that were never allowed in the pre-digital era." Unlike his former conservative allies, Ashcroft was not able to extrapolate from his opposition to Clinton a broader principle of individual liberty that leads to suspicion of government across the board. They had a principle; he turned out to be, first and last, a politician.

Ashcroft's libertarian and evangelical critics after 9/11 were part of a long tradition of antigovernment conservatives that Richard Hofstadter, in his famous 1964 essay, identified with "the paranoid style of American politics"—groups ranging from the anti-Masonic movement, the nativist and anti-Catholic movement, the John Birch Society, and, on the left, the Black Muslims. As Hofstadter defined it, the central preoccupation of the paranoid style "is that of a vast and sinister conspiracy, a gigantic and yet subtle machinery of influence set in motion to undermine and destroy a way of life."[8] Since Hofstadter wrote, this tradition has been associated most famously with the antigovernment wing of the Republican Party, which culminated in its most extreme form in the Oklahoma City bombing. But in its more admirable strains, it has been at the foundation of the principled libertarianism of Armey and Barr. "[N]othing entirely prevents a sound program or a sound issue from being advocated in the paranoid style,"[9] Hofstadter emphasized.

Civil libertarians on the left were more concerned about the rights of noncitizens than their conservative allies were, and more ready to challenge laws and regulations that drew a strong distinction between citizens and aliens. Led by the ACLU, and privacy-advocacy groups such as the Electronic Privacy Information Center and the Center for Democracy and Technology, they focused on challenging the expansion of government secrecy as well as broad new powers to track suspected agents of foreign powers, in the tradition of their opposition to the excesses of the Nixon administration. But on the need to resist the expansion of domestic surveillance, the libertarian left and the libertarian right were in substantial agreement.

During the debate over the USA Patriot Act, libertarians on the left and right made a valiant effort to resist the most draconian provisions in Ashcroft's draft. Far from representing a nuanced response to the challenges posed by Al Qaeda, many of these provisions were rewarmed versions of proposals that had been submitted to Congress by the Clinton Justice Department. Despite their best efforts, however, Armey and Barr were unable to block several expansions of surveillance authority that they had previously resisted. The Patriot Act allows the use of so called "sneak and peek" warrants, which authorize the search of houses without informing the occupants if a judge decides that giving notice would hurt the government's investigation. It permits the Foreign Intelligence Surveillance Court to order roving wiretaps, which follow a suspect rather than being tied to a particular phone or computer. And it gives the government essentially unregulated access to "dialing, routing, addressing, and signaling" information on the Internet—a phrase whose meaning isn't entirely clear but seems to refer to the addresses of the e-mail we send and the Web sites we visit.

Libertarians were better at blocking poorly designed architectures of identity than at proposing constructive alternatives, as their opposition to a national ID card demonstrates. Evangelical fundamentalist Christians, for example, have been among the most vocal opponents of national ID cards based on their literal reading of the Book of Revelation. They believe that the end times before the Battle of Armageddon will include the appearance of a religious tyrant known as the Antichrist. At the same time, these premillennialist Christians believe, a political tyrant will emerge—Revelation calls him "the Beast"—who will unite the ten nations that grew out of the Roman Empire into a new world government.[10] Revelation 13:16–17 warns that the Beast will establish the World Government by requiring everyone "to receive a mark in their right hand, or in their foreheads." Anyone who refuses his "mark" (or "the number of his name," which is 666), will not be permitted to "buy or sell."

Since the mark of the Beast is a passport for citizenship in the One World Government, fundamentalist Christians were

concerned about social security cards when they were first issued, fearing that they might be a sign that the Tribulations had
arrived. For the same reason, they also resisted the bar codes
that are used to scan products in grocery stores: These are seen
as the precursor of a global system of electronic cash that
would put all commerce under the control of the Antichrist.
Throughout the 1980s and 1990s, fundamentalist Christians
were among the most ardent supporters of electronic privacy,
viewing any universal system of identification as a precursor of
the mark of the Beast. They opposed smart cards and other
portable forms of universal identification, out of fear that banks
in the future would argue that cards could be stolen but marks
could not, and therefore would require the codes to be placed
directly on our hands.[11]

Whether or not their objections to government surveillance
had religious roots, libertarian conservatives and liberals were
more willing to oppose systems of identification than to demand
that they be designed in ways that could protect liberty as
well as security. When asked whether he might consider a well-
designed ID card that could increase individuals' control about
how much of themselves to reveal to government, Barr's
instinctive suspicion of government made him reject the suggestion out of hand. "My concern is with surrendering any sem-
blance of privacy whatsoever to the government," he said. "A
national ID, a computer chip, would close off any remaining
avenue for personal privacy." After 9/11, in short, the battle between the antigovernment libertarians and the pro-executive
technopositivists was a recipe for stalemate, not for a pragmatic
balance between liberty and security.

Moderates in the House and Senate were further hampered

in their efforts to seek a middle ground by a lack of familiarity with the technologies in question. Maria Cantwell of Washington State, for example, was perhaps the most technologically savvy member of the Senate. (She complained that congressional rules prohibited her from taking her BlackBerry wireless communicator onto the Senate floor but allowed her to use a spittoon.) Cantwell learned about the importance of Internet privacy as an executive for RealNetworks, which markets one of the most popular Internet music players. In 1999, RealNetworks got into trouble when privacy advocates noticed that the player could send information to RealNetworks about the music each user downloaded. RealNetworks had the capability to match this data with a Globally Unique Identifier, or GUID, that exposed the user's identity. Although RealNetworks insisted that it had never, in fact, matched the music data with the GUID, the company was eager to avoid a public relations disaster, and so it quickly disabled the GUID. The experience helped turn Cantwell into a crusader for privacy, but her time in the Senate made her more pessimistic that her colleagues in Congress had the understanding or inclination to regulate technology in a meaningful way.

"What I don't think people realize is that we are just at the tip of the iceberg," she told me. "I think they're trying to be prescriptive on some very basic things, not understanding the world that's yet to come. I try to explain some of the new technology to my colleagues"—by which she meant her fellow senators. "You're going to be able to be driving and say, 'Hey, take me to the nearest Starbucks,' and they all think that's great. And then I say, 'But it also might be stored in a database that may also be able to track where you were at two o'clock in the morning.'" Cantwell worried that her Senate colleagues were so swept up in the search for a technological solution to our security problems that regulating access to databases and profiling systems wasn't on their agenda. "Databases can become a threat in themselves if you don't think through the right safeguards," she said. "People are getting enamored with the power of the technology and not thinking through the privacy issues and how they might apply."

As it happened, the debate over homeland security progressed along the lines that Cantwell predicted. Two moderate Democratic senators, John Edwards of North Carolina and Charles Schumer of New York, proposed to create a bipartisan commission that would evaluate new surveillance technologies and make recommendations about how they might be designed in ways that protect privacy and security at the same time. Recognizing that "different investigative technologies and methods can achieve the same security goals in ways that have substantially different impacts on individual rights," the bill authorized the commission to study the range of design choices presented by Internet surveillance, data mining, surveillance cameras, X-ray body scans, and biometrics. The commission was directed to identify standards and procedures for selecting and operating the technologies in ways that met the needs of national security and law enforcement "in the manner that best preserves the personal dignity, liberty and privacy of individuals within the United States." But the bill died in the Senate: Because of the polarized politics of homeland security, the Democrats could find no Republican to cosponsor it.

Nevertheless, after creating the new Office of Homeland Security, a group of moderate Republicans and Democrats joined their more libertarian colleagues in repudiating new demands by the president for expanded surveillance authority. They also expressed interest in creating oversight mechanisms that would check the most dramatic executive excesses in the future. What would these oversight mechanisms look like? Congress might try to create alternatives to the kinds of protections for privacy that used to be provided by bureaucratic and technological inefficiencies. During the twentieth century, domestic surveillance was limited by the fact that records were stored in different places, making it hard for local police officials, for example, to check their records against the FBI's watch lists. But after 9/11, these bureaucratic, technological, and legal barriers on information sharing began to break down. The Department of Homeland Security and the USA Patriot Act were based on the principle that government agencies should be able to share and analyze personal information about American citizens and aliens without legal and technological limits. After 9/11, lawmakers became addicted to removing the legal and technological "stovepipes," to use the Washington jargon, that prevented information sharing at the end of the twentieth century. In creating the new Department of Homeland Security, Congress gave federal agents increased authority to share criminal evidence obtained in grand jury investigations with domestic intelligence investigators and to share intelligence information with state and local officials. In the USA Patriot Act, similarly, Congress gave the president new surveillance powers to investigate all crimes, not just terrorist crimes, and it increased the ability of law enforcement agencies to share intercepts of tele-

phone and Internet conversations and other information gathered in ordinary criminal investigations with the CIA, National
Security Administration, and other federal agencies.[12]

Many civil libertarians like bureaucratic inefficiencies, which
they consider the best way of protecting liberty. But there is, in
fact, nothing inherently desirable about preserving inefficiencies, and there are obvious security benefits to minimizing
them. Some of the most notable law enforcement successes
after 9/11—such as the arrest of suspected terrorist cells in
Lackawanna, New York—were aided by the sharing of information among state and federal officials. But as the machine of
government becomes more efficient, Congress needs to think
creatively about ways of reconstructing, through law and technology, the kind of privacy protections that the inefficiencies
used to guarantee. One possibility for a legal solution is what
might be called the "control use" model, suggested by William
Stuntz of Harvard Law School. Stuntz argues that surveillance
authority and information sharing among federal agencies is
perfectly defensible if—and only if—the government can use
the new authority to prosecute only the most serious crimes
and is prohibited from using, sharing, or leaking evidence of
low-level crimes.[13] Stuntz suggests that the executive branch
could strike a bargain with Congress: It gets expanded surveillance authority, but only if it agrees to use the authority to
prosecute terrorists and not ordinary criminals. Stuntz would
limit the list of crimes that could be prosecuted based on evidence produced by data-mining or foreign intelligence searches
to the most serious offenses—terrorism, murder, kidnapping,
rape, and child molestation. In the epilogue, I will suggest an
alternative vision of the "control use" model that would allow

the police to use evidence of lower-level crimes discovered in the course of national security investigations but not general dataveillance.

But regardless of what kind of use limitations are proposed, Congress's experience with the Title III wiretapping law suggests that limitations are unlikely to be adopted or maintained for very long. In 1968, Congress decided that because of the serious threat to privacy that wiretaps posed, they could be justified for twenty-six of the most serious crimes, such as treason, espionage, and crimes of violence. Nearly thirty years later, political pressure had expanded the list of crimes serious enough to justify a wiretap by nearly threefold; and in 1996, 71 percent of all the wiretaps authorized involved drug crimes rather than crimes against the state.[14] In light of the incessant public demands for Congress to prove its mettle by continuing to expand the list of federal crimes, it seems hard to imagine that Congress would agree to impose restrictions on the list for very long.

A more promising model, as I'll suggest in the epilogue, is congressional oversight of surveillance technologies, of the kind that Congress imposed in the USA Patriot Act on the Carnivore e-mail search program. With its nascent suspicion of executive overreaching, Congress is relatively well equipped to ensure that surveillance technologies operate within the boundaries of the law. And the history of privacy regulations in the twentieth century suggests that Congress has tended to take the lead in regulating surveillance technologies, while judges have struggled to keep up with a rapidly changing technological landscape. Since the 1960s, Congress has passed more than a dozen important laws protecting privacy, ranging from Title III, the wiretapping statute, to the Foreign Intelligence Surveillance Act, regulating the surveillance of suspected agents of foreign powers. These laws have provided far more extensive privacy protections than those the Supreme Court said were constitutionally required. In the wiretapping act, for example, the Court said that the Fourth Amendment to the Constitution prohibited only government eavesdropping; but Congress decided to regulate private snoopers as well. The regulation of e-mail privacy followed a similar pattern: Congress passed a comprehensive regulation of e-mail in 1986; nearly twenty years later, the courts still have not decided whether or how stored e-mail is regulated by the Constitution. "Congress has proven itself the most important branch of government in the area of privacy," writes the cyberspace scholar Orin Kerr.[15]

The courts, by contrast, have been less willing to defend privacy and have generally deferred to popular opinion. When presented with stark claims about the unilateral power of the executive, it's true that judges were no less quick than Congress to defend their own prerogatives. For example, in the case of Yaser Esam Hamdi, a twenty-one-year-old American citizen seized on the battlefield in Afghanistan and then locked in the navy brig in Norfolk, the U.S. Court of Appeals for the Fourth Circuit refused to embrace what it called the "sweeping proposition" of the Bush administration—namely that, "with no meaningful judicial review, any American citizen alleged to be an enemy combatant could be detained indefinitely without charges or counsel on the government's say-so."[16] It did, however, endorse the narrower claim that when a citizen is "indisputably seized in an active combat zone abroad," he or she *may* be detained indefinitely on the government's say-so.[17]

But although a few lower-court decisions initially repudiated the executive's demands for increased surveillance authority, many of these decisions were overturned by appellate courts. The Foreign Intelligence Surveillance Court questioned the administration's claim that the USA Patriot Act had torn down the wall between intelligence gathering and law enforcement, but its decision was reversed on appeal. In New Jersey, demand for information on immigrant detainees was granted by a trial court but denied by the state appellate court. An appellate court dismissed a challenge to the government's ability to detain enemy combatants at Guantánamo Bay. Two appellate courts disagreed about whether the government could close immigration deportation hearings to the public. The most dramatic victory for civil libertarians was a decision by a trial court ordering the government to release the names of those detained in the 9/11 investigation, but that decision was reversed on appeal.[18]

What can explain the counterintuitive conclusion that Congress has proved better able than the courts to resist the passions of the moment? The truth is that the vision of heroic judges bravely resisting the currents of popular opinion has always been an American myth. As the Harvard political scientist Robert McCloskey argued in his study of the Supreme Court and popular opinion, first published in the 1960s, the courts over time have tended to follow public opinion rather than to challenge it. "[P]ublic concurrence sets an outer boundary for judicial policy making," McCloskey observed. "Judicial ideas of the good society can never be too far removed from the popular ideas."[19] In the nineteenth and twentieth centuries, the Supreme Court occasionally nudged or tugged at public opinion but more often than not was checked by it. Moreover, on the rare occasions when courts have challenged a deeply felt current in public opinion, they have quickly retreated in the face of a backlash from the political branches. When the Warren Court in the late 1960s, for example, imposed a series of highly controversial procedural rights on the states, such as the exclusionary rule and the Miranda warnings, the Court itself became an issue in presidential politics: Far more than the segregation and school prayer decisions (which were popular with national majorities and only provoked resistance in pockets of the South), the criminal procedure decisions inspired national opposition to the Court that made judicial nominations an issue in presidential politics.[20]

William Stuntz has argued that popular fears inevitably determine the amount of law enforcement authority that judges are willing to give the police. "Most legal restrictions on policing date from the criminal procedure revolution of the 1960s, which itself can be seen as a consequence of the low-crime 1950s," Stuntz writes. "Higher crime rates led to cutbacks in those legal protections in the 1970s and 1980s, just as lower crime rates have led to some expansion in the past few years."[21] To the degree that 9/11 itself was a crime wave, he adds, it is only natural to expect restrictions on law enforcement to contract again in the face of fears of terrorism. The idea that judges could be persuaded to move in the opposite direction contradicts everything we know about the historical relation between popular fears of crime and the judicial response.

Moreover, even if a few judges could be persuaded to dissent from the historical pattern, it's not clear on what constitutional grounds they would stake their case. Conceptions of what is reasonable under the Constitution can never be entirely divorced from popular conceptions of reasonableness. As long as there is no claim that the majority is unfairly ganging up on minorities who can't fend for themselves in the political process, defenders of judicial restraint (and I am one) have traditionally urged courts to defer to the legislature, even when it is acting foolishly or irrationally. The legislature's responses to emotional fears of crime are textbook examples of popular majorities imposing foolish burdens on themselves—adopting poorly designed technologies that threaten liberty and privacy, for example, without bringing us more security. But because all members of the crowd are equally burdened by these pathologies of public opinion, it's hard to argue that judges are needed to save a vulnerable minority from the excesses of the majority. Instead, the impulse to call in the courts reflects the suspicion that the crowd needs to be saved from its own worst impulses, and this is a job that legislators turn out to be better equipped than judges to perform.

Constitutional doctrine, as it has evolved, provides remarkably few restrictions on surveillance technologies that threaten privacy and freedom without protecting security, which makes the need for congressional oversight especially acute. Consider the constitutional dangers posed by mass dataveillance, which occurs when the government searches the private data of millions of innocent citizens in the hope of identifying suspicious patterns. Although Congress rejected the Total Information Awareness data-mining project in its original form, other models of mass dataveillance—such as the advanced Computer Assisted Passenger Screening system—are now being implemented at airports around the world. To guard against broad fishing expeditions, the courts could, in theory, hold that the Fourth Amendment to the Constitution prohibits the government using mass dataveillance to search for evidence of low-level wrongdoing and to prosecute citizens for crimes unrelated to terrorism. Judges in the eighteenth century, after all, ruled that the most invasive searches should be limited to the most dangerous crimes: A private diary, for example, might be seized in connection with a murder investigation but not to prove seditious libel against the Crown. During the twentieth century, however, judges stopped demanding a degree of proportionality between the intrusiveness of a search and the seriousness of a suspected crime. As a result, courts today are not likely to save us from the excesses of personal dataveillance.

This conclusion might seem surprising. Unlike the Carnivore e-mail search program, which targets only suspicious information, mass dataveillance allows the government to search a great deal of innocent information. When the government engages in mass dataveillance to conduct general searches of millions of citizens without cause to believe that a crime has been committed, the searches arguably raise the same dangers in the twenty-first century as the general warrants that the framers of the Fourth Amendment feared in the eighteenth century. Dataveillance, like a general warrant, gives the government essentially unlimited discretion to search through masses of personal information in search of suspicious activity, without specifying in advance the people, places, or things it expects to find. Both general warrants and dataveillance allow fishing expeditions in which the government is trolling for crimes rather than particular criminals, violating the privacy of millions of innocent people in the hope of finding a handful of unknown and unidentified terrorists.

And yet American constitutional law, as it has developed, says that general warrants are unconstitutional, while dataveillance, in most circumstances, is perfectly legal. This jarring conclusion results from the fact that our law of unreasonable searches and seizures originally relied on conceptions of private property to protect privacy. If a search invaded a protected space, like the home, then it was presumptively unreasonable. But once personal information, such as diaries, financial data, letters, and health-care information, began to be stored outside the home, in electronic databases, judges struggled in vain to protect it from general searches by the government. In a series of cases in the 1970s and 1980s, the Supreme Court held that citizens have no reasonable expectation of privacy in information that they have turned over to third parties, such as bank records and telephone dialing information.[22] Although dataveillance, in some ways, reveals even more personal information to the state than a general warrant does, our courts have refused to recognize dataveillance as a search at all, merely because it takes place outside the home.

American courts have been similarly slow to recognize the threat to privacy posed by systems of ubiquitous surveillance in public. The test of whether an unreasonable search has occurred, the Court held in the 1960s, was whether an individual has a subjective expectation of privacy that society is prepared to accept as reasonable.[23] Although initially hailed as a victory for privacy, it soon became clear that this test was circular. People's subjective expectations of privacy reflect the privacy they subjectively experience, and as electronic surveillance in public became more intrusive and more pervasive, it lowered people's objective expectation of privacy as well, with a corresponding diminution of constitutional protections. Following this circular logic, the Court held in the 1970s and 1980s that people have little objective expectation of privacy in public places, even when their movements are observed by technologically enhanced searches (such as helicopters flying over the backyard), because all of us have to assume the risk that our movements in public might be observed. Carried to its logical conclusion, this reasoning would eviscerate privacy by allowing the government to place a camera on each citizen's shoulder to track all of his or her movements in public. This is the characteristic of a police state, not a free society; but the Court seemed unable to distinguish between the risk that a stranger might observe us in passing and the risk that the government might bug us twenty-four hours a day.

The federal government is currently prohibited from centralizing and analyzing large amounts of personal data, but these legal restrictions often don't apply to the analysis of data that are stored in private databases. The government, as a result, has access to increasing amounts of personal information that has been legally collected by commercial data warehouses such as ChoicePoint, which specializes in sorting and packaging more than 10 billion records, indexed by social security number, that have been obtained from marketers, private detectives, and credit card bureaus.[24] From private corporations, state agents can obtain our telephone records, bank records, cable TV records, and credit card records. From our employers and Internet service providers, they can obtain the e-mail we send and the Internet addresses we browse. From credit card reporting agencies, they can obtain detailed reports about our opinions, buying habits, reading habits, and medical prescriptions. After 9/11, this trend increased, as the FBI, without a subpoena or court order, requested records from business; companies that had previously been concerned about appearing to violate the privacy of their customers turned over the information without complaint. In the wake of the terrorist attacks, several large financial companies agreed to turn over information to the FBI.[25]

Mass dataveillance, as I suggested in the prologue, poses at least three distinct dangers: It creates a danger of unlimited bureaucratic discretion, encouraging officials to troll for low-level crimes. It makes it hard for individuals to clear their names or escape their past. And it is a technology of classification and exclusion that limits people's opportunities based on their perceived trustworthiness. But according to the courts, these dangers, however troubling, do not rise to the level of violating constitutional rights. Let's consider each of these three dangers in turn.

First, there is the danger of unsupervised discretion when state agents are free to scan a great deal of innocent activity and then prosecute people for low-level crimes. The British experience with CCTV shows the danger of a snooping society, in which state officials use the threat of terrorism as a pretext for maintaining constant surveillance of society as a whole. Trolling for low-level forms of social disorder allows state officers to reserve for themselves the power to pick individuals out of the crowd and to punish them for relatively minor crimes that would otherwise go unpunished. Although this sort of ubiquitous surveillance is associated in totalitarian societies with Big Brotherism, it's perhaps more accurate, in societies that have traditionally been suspicious of centralized authority, such as England and America, to worry more about the costs of unchecked bureaucratic discretion. In a society in which all personal data are transparent, and many forms of low-level disorder are illegal, state authorities have tremendous discretion to pick and choose among offenses and offenders.

The danger of giving the police unlimited discretion to troll for low-level crimes that can then be linked to certain individuals or groups is, of course, the basic objection to racial profiling. As William Stuntz has argued, racial profiling on the highways of America is essentially unregulated because of two related developments in the law of unreasonable searches and seizures. First, the Supreme Court has said that the police can arrest a citizen who is guilty of any crime, even a very trivial crime. The leading case is *Atwater v. City of Lago Vista*,[26] where the Court rejected the claim that driving without a seat belt was too minor an infraction to justify hauling a suburban mother off to the police station in handcuffs. Second, the Court has said that as long as an officer has the legal authority to search and seize a citizen, his or her actual motive for doing so is irrelevant. In *Whren v. United States*,[27] the Court held that the police permissibly stopped two black teenagers for turning without signaling; it didn't matter that the police used the traffic stop as a pretext for allowing them to search for drugs. "Taken together, *Atwater* and *Whren* allow police officers to use trivial 'crimes' like minor traffic violations as an excuse to detain and search people whom they suspect of more serious offenses," Stuntz writes. "In legal terms, the debate about racial profiling on the highways is largely a debate about the merits of these two rules. With them, officers can select a few speed-limit violators out of the large universe of such violators (all drivers speed) and stop them in order to search for drugs—and that course of action is perfectly legal. Without this pair of rules, such behavior would be a great deal harder to justify."[28]

Before 9/11, both of these legal rules were controversial. Racial profiling of African American drivers in an effort to find drugs seemed so unfair—its benefits so minor and its social costs so high—that even John Ashcroft, the Republican attorney general, promised to eradicate the practice in America. Moreover, the Supreme Court's 5–4 *Atwater* decision, which held that the intrusiveness of a search or seizure need not have any relation to the seriousness of the crime being investigated, was remarkably unconvincing. In his opinion for the Court, Justice David Souter claimed that in the eighteenth century, officers could arrest anyone they had probable cause to believe had committed a crime, no matter how minor. Souter's historical claims were dubious, and there is a strong argument that the historical evidence actually supports the opposite conclusion: In the eighteenth century, arrests without a warrant for minor offenses were generally unlawful, except in some well-defined categories of minor offenses where there was an unusual need for a prompt arrest.[29] The eighteenth-century framers were so concerned about executive discretion, in other words, that they insisted on limiting the most intrusive searches and seizures to the most serious crimes. But after 9/11, the increased sympathy for law enforcement makes it even less likely that judges will insist on resurrecting constitutional limits on executive discretion to search and seize.

The second danger that dataveillance presents is the danger that individuals will find it harder to escape their past in a world of permanent and increasingly transparent data mining and profiling, like the low-level shoplifters who could set off biometric alerts when they tried to enter the British Borders bookstore. But the courts have suggested that the Constitution provides no remedy for that harm, either. A citizen who has been permanently flagged in a secret database has been branded, in a sense, as infamous. But courts are not likely to help the stigmatized individuals clear their names. The constitutional guarantee of "equal protection of the laws" has been interpreted to forbid the state from intentionally discriminating against citizens based on immutable characteristics, such as race or gender; but the personal information in a data profile is based on our past behavior rather than our immutable attributes, on what we have done rather than who we are.

Perhaps the closest analogies to an intrusive computer profile or system of dataveillance are the Internet sex crime registries that every state in the Union adopted after the murder of a child named Megan Kanka in 1994. The laws, ostensibly designed to protect public safety, typically require all sex offenders, both violent and nonviolent, to enroll in a public registry that is on the Internet. In 2003, the Supreme Court rejected constitutional challenges to Megan's Law in Alaska and Connecticut filed by two convicts who insisted that the government had unfairly tarred them as dangerous sex offenders without giving them a chance to prove that, in fact, they posed no threat to the community. An earlier ruling from 1976 had upheld a decision by a local police department to circulate to local merchants flyers displaying photographs of "active shoplifters."

Although the police department had indeed stigmatized the shoplifters, Justice William Rehnquist held, they weren't deprived of any legally protected rights, such as the right to buy alcohol or to travel.[30] In the same spirit, the Court held that the convicted sex offenders publicized on an Internet database, like former shoplifters, may have been stigmatized, but they were not deprived of any legal rights. As Justice Ruth Bader Ginsburg noted in a dissenting opinion, however, the man who was identified as a former sex offender on the Internet had experienced the indignity of having negative information published about himself without any opportunity to put himself in context by posting positive information, such as the fact that a lower court had granted him custody of his young daughter on the grounds that he had been rehabilitated after serving his time. The court found that he had a "very low risk of reoffending" and "is not a pedophile."[31] But these highly relevant facts were omitted on the Internet sex registry, which lumped him together with far more dangerous characters.

Like an Internet sex offenders registry, a data-profiling system that flags former shoplifters or former deadbeat dads every time they try to board a plane arguably stigmatizes them without punishing them. Although the shoplifters would be embarrassed every time they were singled out for special searches, as long as they weren't prohibited from boarding the plane or entering the building, courts might well conclude that they weren't deprived of legal rights by the disclosure of truthful information. Nevertheless, it's hard not to have sympathy for the former shoplifters or former deadbeat dads who have been unfairly stigmatized by the state for low-level crimes long after their debt to society has been discharged. A "stigma" is a "mark or

token of infamy, disgrace, or reproach,"[32] and a profiling system that made it impossible for Americans to escape from their
past misdeeds could clearly stigmatize them in ways disproportionate to their original offenses.

The courts are also unlikely to provide a remedy for the
third and final harm caused by dataveillance: discriminatory
classification of citizens based on electronic profiles. To the degree that dataveillance leads to what David Lyon calls "digital
discrimination," it is not likely to be the kind of intentional
discrimination that violates the Constitution. Risk profiles are
based on a broad array of personal characteristics, and only a
handful of them—race or religion, for example—are constitutionally suspicious. And courts have held repeatedly that as
long as race or religion is only one factor in a broad profile that
includes constitutionally unobjectionable data as well—such as
financial information and travel destination—then the profile
doesn't violate the Constitution.[33] The fact that the discriminatory effects of risk profiles may be far more sweeping than
those of racial profiling probably reduces their constitutional
vulnerability: If everyone is sorted into risk categories, targeted
citizens can't object that they are being singled out for special
discrimination.

As we will see in the epilogue, it's possible to imagine various models for technological and legal oversight of the most
extreme and invasive forms of surveillance, data mining, and
profiling. I've argued that congressional oversight, subject to
political accountability, offers the most promising avenue for
regulation: Despite the polarized nature of the legislative debate, Congress has proved more willing than the courts to balance the executive's demand for security above all against more

moderate alternatives. But architectures that protect liberty and security can't be imposed on the public against its will; in order to strike a reasonable balance between privacy and security, the public would have to care about privacy in a sustainable way, and it's not clear that we really do. We expose details of our personal lives on talk shows and on the Internet, and we enjoy watching others expose themselves in a similarly exhibitionistic way on reality TV. Far from trying to master our fears, we wallow in them by watching TV shows like *Fear Factor*, where participants are forced to reenact their most dreaded anxieties; and we crave similar alarmism from cable TV news, which has become like a 24/7 version of a reality show, pandering fear as a form of voyeuristic entertainment.

When people say they care about privacy, in short, what they really mean is that they want control over the conditions of their personal exposure; and what they really fear isn't loss of privacy but loss of control. Americans are perfectly happy to violate their own privacy, and those of strangers, as long as they have an illusion of control over the conditions under which the violation occurs. As we will see in the next chapter, the same people who say they are concerned about having their privacy violated by the state are all too willing to expose personal information in exchange for an elusive and fleeting feeling of security and emotional connection. Given this unfortunate dynamic, in which the crowd demands exposure and individuals are happy to oblige, it seems unrealistic to expect that citizens will demand protections for the privacy of others when they perceive an immediate security benefit for themselves. A society of anxious exhibitionists who fear loss of control above all will choose security over privacy every time.

CHAPTER FIVE

Identity Crisis

AFTER 9/11, THE MOST CELEBRATED RITUAL OF MOURN-
ing was *The New York Times'* Portraits of Grief. For months
after the attack, the *Times* published more than 1,800 sketches
of those who died in the collapse of the World Trade Center.
Not designed as obituaries in the traditional sense—at 200
words, there was no space for a full accounting of the lives that
had been cut short—the portraits were offered up as "brief, informal, and impressionistic, often centered on a single story or
idiosyncratic detail," intended not "to recount a person's ré-
sumé, but rather to give a snapshot of each victim's personality,
of a life lived."[1] They were intended to be democratic—showing
the personal lives of janitors as well as chief executives. Above
all, they attempted to recognize the victims as distinctive individuals, each distinguished from the crowd. "One felt, looking
at those pages every day, that real lives were jumping out at
you," said Paul Auster, the novelist, when interviewed by the
Times about the profiles. "We weren't mourning an anonymous mass of people, we were mourning thousands of indi-

viduals. And the more we knew about them, the more we could wrestle with our own grief."[2]

Although public criticism of the Portraits of Grief was hard to detect during the months of their publication, a few dissident voices emerged after the series came to an end. More than 80 percent of the victims' families agreed to talk to the *Times,* but a handful of them later complained that the portraits had failed to capture the people they had known. In an eloquent essay in *The American Scholar,* the literary critic Thomas Mallon echoed this criticism, arguing that in the process of trying to individualize their subjects, the Portraits of Grief had managed to homogenize them instead. "To read the Portraits one would believe that work counted for next to nothing, that every hard-charging bond trader and daredevil fireman preferred—and managed—to spend more time with his family than at the office," Mallon wrote.

Unlike the real victims, who had a share of "bad marriages, maxed-out credit cards, and type-A heartbreak," the "smile-button cyborgs of the *Times*" were bland abstractions. "Anyone depressed over his weight became a 'gentle giant,' " Mallon observed, "and every binge drinker was the life of the party." The titles of the portraits encapsulated their sentimentalism, from "The Joys of Fatherhood" and "Prankster with a Heart" to "Mr. Generosity." American obituaries, to a certain extent, tend to obey the convention of speaking well of the dead (British obituaries are far nastier), but the Portraits of Grief were not successful on their own terms: Instead of recognizing the public achievements of lives that had reached some kind of fulfillment, the portraits instead trivialized their subjects by emphasizing one or two private hobbies or quirks. As a result, any genuine achievements or complexity of personality were airbrushed away in the narrative effort to reduce each person to a single, memorable, and democratically accessible detail. "If Mayor Rudolph Giuliani had perished in the attacks, as he nearly did," Mallon concluded, "he would be remembered in the Portraits as a rabid Yankee fan who sometimes liked to put on lipstick."[3]

The homogenizing effects of the Portraits of Grief were inherent in the project itself. The *Times* instructed its reporters to convey a sense of the victims as distinct individuals by extracting from conversations with their families a single representative detail about their lives that would give readers the illusion of having known them. In each case, complexity and accuracy had to be sacrificed to the narrative imperative of finding a memorable quirk of personality with which the audience could quickly identify. A friend of mine who wrote some of the early portraits for the *Times* describes how invasive the project seemed as he interviewed the victims' families in the weeks after the attack. "One of the mothers was crying hysterically and telling me her son liked cigars, and all I could think was: How much does he like cigars?; I needed more to make that detail work," he recalled. "The whole thing seemed incredibly reductionistic."

But the Portraits of Grief were not designed to do justice to the victims in all of their complexity. They were designed as a form of therapy for the families of the victims and as a source of emotional connection for the readers of the *Times*. They aspired to give all Americans the illusion of identifying with the victims, therefore allowing them to feel that they themselves had somehow been touched by the horrific event. What was flattened out in this juggernaut of democratic connection was the individuality of the victims themselves.

This flattening resulted from a broader demand: the Naked Crowd's insistence on emotionally memorable images at the expense of genuine human individuality. The crowd, which thinks in terms of images rather than arguments, demands a sense of emotional connection with everyone who catches its fleeting attention. This means that everyone who is subject to the scrutiny of the crowd—from celebrities to political candidates to the families of terrorists' victims—will feel pressure to parcel out bits of personal information in order to allow unseen strangers to experience a sense of vicarious identification. Because the crowd has a short attention span, the personal information that is offered up for its consumption must be vivid, simplified, and easy to remember. But revealing one or two personal details to strangers is inevitably a trivializing experience that leads us to be judged out of context. (As a harrowing parlor game, my wife and I imagined portraits of grief for each other. I became "an ebullient ham who had a weakness for champagne and musical comedy"; she morphed into "a wise-cracking bassoon player who enjoyed organizing and tidying up.") It's impossible to know someone on the basis of snippets of information; genuine knowledge is something that can be achieved only slowly, over time, behind a shield of privacy, with the handful of people to whom we've chosen to reveal ourselves whole. And even those who know us best may not know us in all of our complicated dimensions. The mother who told the *Times* that her forty-seven-year-old son was "proud to be a mama's boy"[4] failed to recognize that the man may have been a mama's boy to her, but not to the girlfriends that she confessed she didn't care for, and he may have preferred to be remembered for his own reality rather than hers.

The homogenization wrought by the Portraits of Grief was not unique to the tragedy of 9/11. It is a symptom of the identity crisis that Americans are experiencing as they attempt to negotiate the challenges of the Omnipticon—a world in which more and more citizens are subject to the scrutiny of strangers. The challenges of interacting with strangers have increased the pressures on Americans to trade privacy for an illusory sense of security and connection, turning many of us into virtual portraits of grief. The sociologist Anthony Giddens has described the ways that citizens in a risk society can no longer rely on tradition or fixed hierarchies to establish their identity or to give them reliable guidance about whom to trust in a society of strangers. Confused and anxious about status in a world where status is constantly shifting, we feel increasing pressure to expose details of our personal lives to strangers in order to win their trust, and we demand that they expose themselves in return in order to win our trust. "Trust—in a person or in a system, such as a banking system—can be a means of coping with risk, while acceptance of risk can be a means of generating trust,"[5] Giddens writes. In the past, intimate relationships of trust—such as marriage, friendship, and business associations—were based on rigidly controlled status hierarchies, which brought with them codes of expected behaviors: You could behave one way with your wife and another with your servant and another with your boss, because you had no doubt where you stood in relationship to each of them, and where they stood in relation to you. Today, by contrast, intimacy and trust are increasingly obtained not by shared experiences or fixed social status but by self-revelation: People try to prove their trustworthiness by revealing details of their personal lives to prove that they have nothing to hide before a crowd whose gaze is turned increasingly on all the individuals that compose it. Just as corporations and governments are increasingly mining the personal data of individuals to decide whom to trust, so individuals are voluntarily exposing their own personal information in order to establish their trustworthiness. In this chapter, I want to explore why it is that American anxiety about identity has led us to value exposure over privacy, and why this should make us even more skeptical that Americans will calmly evaluate the costs and benefits of new technologies of surveillance and exposure that have been developed in the private sector and are now being appropriated by the government. Why, in short, are we so eager to become members of the Naked Crowd?

A world where individuals have to prove their trustworthiness and value every day before the crowd, choosing among an infinite range of lifestyles, behaviors, clothes, and values, is inevitably a world that creates great anxiety about identity. Rather than conforming to preexisting social roles, individuals are expected to find their true selves and constantly to market themselves to a skeptical world. Successful individuals are those who sustain a coherent narrative throughout their entire careers, but the possibility of failure is present every day. (You are, in the eyes of the crowd, only as good as your next book, or next hit, or next deal.) Even in an age of terror, the dangers of fading out are greater than those of being blown up. In the 1950s, Erich Fromm wrote about the "marketing orientation" of the American self, in which "man experiences himself as a thing to be employed successfully on the market. . . . His sense of value depends on his success: on whether he can sell himself favorably. . . . If the individual fails in a profitable investment of himself, he feels that *he* is a failure; if he succeeds, *he* is a success."[6] Fromm worried that the marketed personality, whose precarious sense of self-worth was entirely dependent on the fickle judgments of the market, would be racked by alienation and anxiety.

The Internet has vastly increased the opportunities for individuals to subject themselves to the demands of the personality market, resulting in ever-increasing confusion and anxiety about how much of ourselves to reveal to strangers. The logic of Fromm's marketed self is being extended into a virtual world where the easiest way to attract the attention and win the trust of strangers is to establish an emotional connection with them by projecting a consistent, memorable, and trustworthy image. In an ideal relationship of trust, self-revelation should be reciprocal. In the age of the Internet, however, we are increasingly forced to interact with strangers whom we will never meet face-to-face. As a result, individuals find themselves in more and more situations where they feel pressure to reveal details of their personal lives without being able to gauge the audience's reaction. But the quest for attention from and emotional connection with strangers is fraught with peril.[7]

In 2000, for example, Laurence Tribe, the constitutional scholar from Harvard Law School, posted a personal statement on his family's Web page. "I'm Larry," Tribe wrote. "I love brilliant magenta sunsets, unagi, Martin Amis' 'Time's Arrow,' the fish tank at MGH, T. S. Eliot's 'Love Song of J. Alfred Prufrock,' eating, my stairmaster, looking at the ocean, dreaming about impossible things, *New Yorker* cartoons, the twist in a short story, *The Hotel New Hampshire,* good (and even not-so-good) movies, re-reading the *Great Gatsby* and *Ethan Frome,* and Monet and Vermeer." Several Web sites devoted to media gossip posted links mocking Tribe's statement for displaying the overly intimate tones of a personal ad. Embarrassed by the public reaction, Tribe tried to remove the statement, but one of the media-gossip sites resurrected it from the archives of Google, the popular Internet search engine. Tribe was then ridiculed more for his attempt to cover his tracks than for his initial act of self-exposure. "The website itself was a thing our son helped Carolyn and me put together one Christmas," Tribe e-mailed me later, reflecting on his experience. "I was having fun letting my hair down, as it were, in just chatting about myself as unself-consciously as I could, not giving much of a thought to who might read it but probably assuming, naively it now seems, that it wouldn't really be of interest to anybody. When I learned that people were finding it a source of public amusement, I do admit to being nonplused and unsure of what to do."

Tribe's understandable error shows how hard it is to strike a decent balance between personal disclosure and the projection of a consistent image, especially on the Internet. A public relations agent might have explained to Tribe that in a world of short attention spans, the public doesn't have the patience to understand individuals in all of their complexities: It expects them to be predictable, like a brand of packaged breakfast cereal. "In order to exclude undesired and undesirable aspects," Daniel Boorstin wrote in *The Image,* "an image must be simpler than the object it represents."[8] The Tyler Professor of Constitutional Law, in other words, isn't supposed to depict himself on a StairMaster. Like the Portraits of Grief, a successful act of self-revelation on the Web is supposed to simplify and homogenize the personality that it is attempting to market, presenting an image to the crowd that is intelligible, consistent, and easily remembered.

Many citizens, of course, don't care if they embarrass themselves before strangers on the Internet, as the proliferation of personal Web pages shows. It is now commonplace on these Web pages to reveal hobbies, favorite foods and music, and pictures of children, in an effort to create an illusion of intimacy. Even the most personal moments of life, such as weddings, are now being posted on the Web for public consumption. A Web site called theknot.com contains an archive of "real weddings," in which the bride and groom enumerate every moment of their courtship, their vows, their favorite music and food, and sometimes even their honeymoon. Along the same lines, the *Times'* wedding section now reflects the same pressure for emotional connection with strangers as did the Portraits of Grief. Not long ago, the *Times* began asking couples who submit wedding announcements to describe how they met. Many announcements now include detailed and highly personal accounts of the bungled advances, e-mail messages gone astray, and initial ambivalence overcome by perseverance that make up the messy reality of many courtships. But although they are designed to convey a sense of the couples as individuals, many of the details seem mundane and formulaic instead. The more exhibitionistic offerings, in fact, quickly become ridiculous: The unique experience of love and courtship is too intimate and specific to be easily conveyed to strangers. The private moments offered up for public consumption tend to be generic tropes of democratic informality that, like the Portraits of Grief, have a homogenizing effect. Instead of the beginning of a romantic partnership, one often has the impression of watching a particularly excruciating episode of *The Dating Game.*

And then there are the reality TV shows, which represent the most absurd examples of the application of the values of the public-opinion society to the most intimate activities of life. A model of this genre is the FOX TV show *Married by America,* in which participants agree to marry, sight unseen, whomever the audience selects as their mate. The male and female suitors are required to make their case to the television audience by revealing their most intimate secrets and presenting their connubial qualifications like political candidates. What's striking about the purportedly embarrassing revelations is how generic they are: In early episodes, women confessed that they were oversexed—one had posed for *Playboy*—and men confessed that they were undersexed—one was a virgin until he graduated from college. The homogenizing yet titillating tone of the program pressured all the women to conform to men's fantasies of fecundity and all the men to conform to women's fantasies of fidelity. Instead of conveying a sense of these people as individuals, the democratic exposure made them merge into an amorphous mass.

One way of understanding privacy is not whether we choose to expose personal information in public—we all do at different times and places—but the ease with which we can return to being private. The Internet, however, is complicating our ability to negotiate the boundary between public and private, making it hard to recover a private self that has been voluntarily exposed. Consider the proliferation of Weblogs, or blogs—personal Internet journals that often combine political musings with intimate disclosures about daily life. There are more than half a million, according to the latest estimate.[9] Some are devoted exclusively to public affairs, while others are nothing more than published diaries. A site called Diarist.net collects more than 5,000 journals from self-styled "on-line exhibitionists." Often, these diaries are virtually unreadable examples of self-display, dreary accounts of daily navel gazing whose primary function seems to be therapeutic. But they reflect a common but treacherous error: that thoughts appropriate to reveal to friends and intimates are also appropriate to reveal to the world. As a result, the diaries and Weblogs lurk in cyberspace, ready to be resurrected in the future by fellow citizens or government officials in ways that we may later regret.

For example, a blogger called Dooce identifies herself as "that girl who lost her job because of her website."[10] If you follow the link, you will learn that Dooce used her blog to ridicule her boss in the most childish manner, making fun of her tendency to talk with her hands. After an anonymous tipster e-mailed the company vice president that Dooce had made fun of her boss, the blogger was fired. "At what point does my personal website, regardless of what I've published on the site, affect my professional life?" Dooce complained. Dooce seemed not to understand that ranting on a blog is a public rather than a private act: In another exhibitionistic turn, she ridiculed her Mormon parents on her blog, and then professed to be shocked and distressed when they were devastated by her anti-Mormon diatribe. And far from being genuinely remorseful, Dooce boasts about the episode on her home page in the same way that she boasted about being fired. Dooce is a less sympathetic figure than Laurence Tribe, whose struggles with the boundaries between the public and private had an appealing sincerity. But both of them found that these boundaries were less permeable, and harder to recover, than they had expected.

It's possible, of course, to imagine a norm developing that allowed blogs to be considered an intermediate space between the public and private. Perhaps people might eventually agree that it's not proper to discuss in public what they read on a blog, just as it wasn't proper for the servants in eighteenth-century England to report what they learned while serving their masters. But the norms of reticence in eighteenth-century England depended on a rigid social hierarchy that ensured there would be social consequences imposed on inferiors who violated the trust of their betters. In the democratic world of the Omnipticon, in which strangers watch each other, the connections between the watchers and the watched are too diffuse for communal norms to be enforced in a reliable way.

In a pluralistic society, people are and should be free to have different instincts about the proper balance between reticence and self-revelation. If exercises in personal exhibitionism give pleasure to the exhibitionists and an illusory sense of emotional connection for the virtual audience, there's no harm done except to the dignity of the individuals concerned, and that's nobody's business but their own. But the growing pressure to expose ourselves in front of strangers has obvious and important consequences for a democracy's ability to strike a reasonable balance between liberty and security. The ease with which we reveal ourselves to strangers suggests that in the face of widespread anxiety about identity, people are more concerned with the feeling of connection than with the personal and social costs of exposure.

Anxiety about how much of ourselves to reveal to strangers has always been a defining trait of the American character. But the form of the anxiety changed over the course of the nineteenth and twentieth centuries, reflecting changes in society and technology. In his discussion of why Americans were restless in the midst of prosperity, Tocqueville noted that when individuals are all nearly equal, it is very difficult for any one person to distinguish himself from "the uniform crowd that surrounds him and presses against him."[11] The result, he predicted, would be growing anxiety about status in a world where status was constantly shifting.

When Tocqueville came to America in 1831, American society was in transition from a vertical society, in which identity was fixed by birth or social position, to a horizontal society, in which identity was malleable and people were free to choose their identity and to interact on terms of equality.[12] In the eighteenth century, when citizens had no doubt where they stood in the ruthless and inflexible pecking order, interactions among different classes of people could be regulated by a sense of honor. The notion that gentlemen should behave honorably, for example, was an idea that high-status people traditionally used to differentiate themselves from low-status people. In a traditional honor-based society, like the old South, if you were insulted by a social equal, you challenged him to a duel, and if you were insulted by a social inferior, you bludgeoned him with a cane. But under no circumstances would a gentleman sue another gentleman, because the honor code held that an offense against honor could be answered only by a physical attack.

In an honor culture, ritualized disrespect for someone's public face was a serious insult that could be avenged only by a duel. Nose pulling, for example, was known as a "Lieutenant Randolph's outrage" because of a famous incident in 1833 in which Robert Beverly Randolph, a disgraced former naval officer, tried to pull the nose of President Andrew Jackson. Jackson had dismissed Lieutenant Randolph from the navy for financial improprieties that arose under his watch as purser for the U.S.S. *Constitution*. Randolph felt unjustly treated (an investigation found no intentional wrongdoing); and in an effort to avenge his honor, he approached Jackson during the president's visit to Fredericksburg. Randolph then took off his glove and tried to pull the president's nose. The sixty-six-year-old Jackson reacted violently: He grabbed his cane, thrust it at Randolph, and demanded revenge. "Let no man interfere between me and this personal insult," he shouted. Several years later, after Randolph was finally convicted of the assault, Jackson rejected the interference of the court in what he regarded as an affair of honor. He asked President Van Buren to pardon Randolph, citing the wishes of his mother, who had long advised him to "indict no man for assault and battery or sue him for slander."[13]

In the democratizing wave of the Jacksonian era, the old social hierarchies that sustained the honor system began to collapse. For some people to have honor, it was necessary for others not to have it, and this aristocratic premise became hard to sustain in an increasingly egalitarian age. As young men swept from the countryside into the cities, citizens were increasingly forced to transact business with anonymous strangers whose character and family background were impossible to gauge. At a time when people no longer knew their place, there was growing concern about being out of place. Uncertain about their own social status, and that of their neighbors, middle-class Americans in the 1830s developed a special anxiety about being duped or swindled by unscrupulous strangers who posed as respectable citizens. In particular, Americans in the age of Jackson worried about "confidence men" who preyed on innocent citizens. (The term "confidence man" came from a well-dressed New York swindler in the mid–nineteenth century who would approach gentlemen on the street, talk to them briefly, and then ask whether they had the confidence to lend a stranger their watch. When they handed over the watch, he would walk away with it, chuckling.)[14] The national concern about being duped by the false appearances of strangers was reflected in books like Melville's *The Confidence-Man: His Masquerade.*[15]

In the age of Jackson, Americans responded to their fears of being victimized by hypocritical strangers by developing a cult of sincerity. Advice manuals urged respectable young men to establish a good reputation among strangers by cultivating a complete transparency of manner, so that there was a perfect correlation between their outward appearance and their innermost character. Virtuous youths were urged to be as sincere as Adam before the Fall, whose face, as the moralists repeatedly observed, "was the index of his mind." But the cult of sincerity presented a practical problem: Those who disclosed too much about themselves in the wrong context might be taken advantage of by unscrupulous strangers. For this reason, advice manuals urged readers not to reveal themselves indiscriminately in public—"In general, it is the best way to say as little about ourselves, our friends, our books, and our circumstances as possible"[16]—and to reserve their carefully regulated disclosures for more protected settings. In particular, as the historian Karen Halttunen has described, the Victorian parlor was the place that middle-class Americans were encouraged to practice the cult of sincerity—a place where women could limit entrance to those with good reputations, and men could practice the easy, unaffected, but guarded candor that marked them as worthy of trust.

At the beginning of the twenty-first century, the problem of self-identification that vexed the Jacksonians—how much of ourselves should we reveal to strangers?—has become even more acute. In the late nineteenth century, conceptions of personal truthfulness changed in a way that the critic Lionel Trilling described as a change from sincerity to authenticity.[17] By sincerity, Trilling meant the expectation that individuals should avoid duplicity in their dealings with one another: There should be an honest correlation between what is exposed in public and what is felt in private, but not everything that is felt has to be exposed. By authenticity, Trilling meant the expectation that instead of being honest with one another, individuals should be honest with themselves, and should have no compunction about directly exposing strangers to their most intimate emotions. Sincerity requires that whatever is exposed must be true; authenticity requires that everything must be exposed as long as it is deeply felt.

In the age of sincerity, the fine clothes and family crest of the aristocrat were the markers of the self; in the age of authenticity, as the sociologist Peter Berger has noted, "the escutcheons hide the true self. It is precisely the naked man, and even more specifically the naked man expressing his sexuality, who represents himself more truthfully."[18] The motto for the age of sincerity came from the Delphic oracle: Know thyself. The motto for the age of authenticity comes from the therapist: Be thyself.

As self-disclosure became the yardstick of trustworthiness, individuals began to relate to strangers in psychological terms. Politicians, like actors on the stage, came to be judged as trustworthy only if they could convincingly dramatize their own emotions and motivations. "The content of political belief recedes as in public, people become more interested in the content of the politician's life,"[19] Richard Sennett writes. "The modern charismatic leader destroys any distance between his own sentiments and impulses and those of his audience, and so, focusing his followers on his motivations, deflects them from measuring him in terms of his acts."[20] We saw examples of this dynamic in the last political scandal before 9/11, a drama involving a California congressman who had an affair with a young intern who was subsequently murdered. Although there was no evidence linking him to the murder, the man's political career was ended when he went on television to defend himself but then refused to express the emotions that the public expected: Like Coriolanus, he ignored the crowd's demands that he show his emotional wounds, and the crowd reacted to this slight by turning on him in fury. After 9/11, political leaders were careful not to make the same mistake: The president and defense secretary, two buttoned-up WASPs, managed to weep ostentatiously on television, assuring the public that they shared its pain. On the first anniversary of the attacks, a network anchorman solemnly assured the nation that "the president has often remarked that the Bush men are emotional, father and son. So I'm sure we'll see tears, but also a steely resolve." The earnest nod, the brow furrowed by concern, and the well-timed tear are now more important for politicians than traditional skills of oratory.

In *The Image,* Daniel Boorstin explored the way the growth of movies, radio, print, and television had transformed the nature of political authority, which came to be exercised not by the distant and remote hero but instead by the celebrity, whom Boorstin defined as "a person who is known for his well-knownness."[21] "Neither good nor bad," a celebrity is "morally neutral," "the human pseudo-event," who has been "fabricated on purpose to satisfy our exaggerated expectations of human greatness."[22] While the heroes of old exercised authority by being remote and mysterious, modern celebrities exercise authority by being familiar and intelligible, creating the impression—but not the reality—of emotional accessibility. Heroes were distinguished by their achievement, celebrities by their images or trademarks or "name brands." Increasingly, Boorstin wrote, communities, corporations, and nations as well as political leaders were being marketed and measured in terms of their images rather than in terms of external ideals. An image, like a trademark or brand name, had to be believable, vivid, concrete, and, above all, simple and consistent, so that it could easily be remembered by a distracted public. It served its purposes by appealing to the public's emotions rather than its interests. And like trademarks and brand names, images were synthetic: planned, created, and managed for the purpose of making a particular impression. In an age when images were becoming more important than reality, Boorstin lamented the fact that politicians were trying to hold the attention of the crowd by recasting themselves in the mold of celebrities, projecting an image of emotional authenticity through selective self-disclosure. He feared that as synthesized images took the place of complicated human reality, the result would be a proliferation of conformity: Politicians would have to alter their personalities to fit with the images that the crowd expected them to present; and the believability of the image would become more important than the underlying human truth.

Boorstin wrote before the development of the Internet. But as life increasingly takes place in cyberspace, private citizens are now facing some of the same social pressures and technological opportunities as politicians to expose and market themselves to strangers, with similarly homogenizing results. As the Internet has increased the circumstances in which ordinary citizens are forced to present a coherent image to strangers, the methodology of public relations is increasingly being applied to the presentation of the self. Ordinary citizens are now being forced to market themselves like pseudo-events, using techniques that used to be reserved for politicians, corporations, and celebrities. In an eerie fulfillment of Boorstin's fears, business gurus today are urging individuals to project a consistent image to the crowd by creating a personal brand.

The idea of selling people as products began to appear in magazines like *Advertising Age* as early as the 1970s; but the idea of personal branding didn't proliferate until the 1990s, when a series of business books emerged with names like *Brand You, The Personal Branding Phenomenon,* and *Be Your Own Brand: A Breakthrough Formula for Standing Out from the Crowd.* To invent a successful brand, you have to establish trust with strangers, argues the personal-branding guru, Tom Peters. A brand is a "trust mark" that "reaches out with a powerful connecting experience." To connect with colleagues and customers, you have to decide the one thing you want them to know about you and create an "emotional context" by telling stories about yourself. Peters's nostrums are an example of the banalization of Gustave Le Bon, and *Be Your Own Brand* is in the same vein. It defines a personal brand as "a perception or emotion, maintained by somebody other than you, that describes the total experience of having a relationship with you."[23] Like the brand of a corporation or product, personal brands are defined by whether people trust, like, remember, and value you: "Your brand, just like the brand of a product, exists on the basis of a set of perceptions and emotions stored in someone else's head."[24] To create a strong personal brand that makes and maintains an emotional connection with strangers, individuals are advised to be "distinctive, relevant, and consistent."[25]

Distinctiveness means standing for something recognizable, but the branding manuals emphasize that a strong brand is "not the same as morality in the spiritual sense."[26] Like celebrities, personal brands are morally neutral: The convicted mobster John Gotti had a strong brand in the same way that the scandalized silent-film star Fatty Arbuckle did. The goal of the branded self is not to be good or to behave well but to be noticed, to stand out from the crowd. In addition to being distinctive, brands must be "relevant," which is to say, "what they stand for connects to what someone else considers to be important."[27] The branded self is measured ultimately by its success on the market: "To get credit (acknowledgment, acceptance, recognition)," *Be Your Own Brand* urges people to "live their brand's values every day, testing them in the 'marketing place' of personal and professional relationships and watching how others accept or reject those values." Finally, there is the requirement of consistency: Because "people come to believe in a relationship based on the consistency of behaviors they experience or observe," branded individuals are urged to maintain a seamless consistency between their private lives and public image. "If you're cheerful at work, you should be cheerful at home," *Be Your Own Brand* exhorts. "If you have the mettle to hold up under pressure as a parent, you should be a good bet to exhibit the same resilience in the workplace."[28]

To achieve the goals of distinctiveness, relevance, and consistency, branded individuals are urged to simplify the complex characteristics that make up a genuine individual. Following the model of the Portraits of Grief, personal branders urge their clients to write down a list of the adjectives that best describe their personal style and values, and to incorporate three of them in a "personal brand promise" that can easily be remembered. (This is another harrowing parlor game.) For example, a surgeon who says he is "humble, collaborative, and friendly" promises "the discipline to achieve world-class results"; a writer who claims to be "enthusiastic, energetic, and professional" promises "enthusiasm that will make your day." These brand attributes are so abstract and banal that they are impossible to remember, which is why the entire enterprise seems dubious even on its own terms; but they neatly achieve the goal of turning individuals into stereotypes, for the purpose of making them intelligible to strangers with short attention spans.

In *The Lonely Crowd*, his classic study of the American self in the 1950s, the sociologist David Riesman distinguished between the inner-directed individual, who derives his identity from an internal moral gyroscope, and the outer-directed individual, who derives his identity from the expectations of the crowd. By measuring individuals in terms of their success on the personality market, the personal-branding strategy seems at first to be an apotheosis of outer-directedness. But the personal-branding books deny this, emphasizing that successfully branded individuals must first look inward, to discover their authentic selves, and then turn outward, in attempting to market that self to the world. "Trust is built faster and maintained longer when people believe you are being real, not putting on a false front to cover up what's really going on inside of you," the branding manual counsels. "When it comes to relationships, authenticity is what others say they want most from us. We make the most lasting and vivid impressions when people witness us being true to our beliefs, staying in alignment with who and what we really are."[29] The self constructed by the personal branders, then, is an anxious hybrid of Riesman's two types: a form of marketed authenticity in which the self is turned inside out and then sold to the world.

Although the phenomenon of personal-brand management is in its infancy, it represents the logical application of marketing technologies to the most intimate aspects of the self. But its hazards are already becoming evident, and they have to do with the substitution of image-making for genuine individuality. As early as 1997, the *Times* reported that an unhappy bachelor had convened a focus group of the single women who had rejected him. As he watched from behind a one-way mirror, they evaluated his dating performance and offered advice for improvement. Meeting in the studios of a market research company called Focus Suites, where consumers usually gathered to criticize soap or cereal, the women urged him to bolster his confidence and change his wardrobe. "I think it's really alarming that we let a market economy dictate our human relationships," the head of the company told the *Times*. "I think it's much more healthy for the human model to dictate to the business world than for the business model to inform human life."[30]

Allowing public opinion to expand into the recesses of the soul, the entrepreneurs of the self insist that personal branding is a spiritual as well as an economic imperative. Nick Shore, the head of a New York advertising agency called the Way Group, is writing a book called *Who Are You: The Search for Your Authentic Self in Business*. Over the phone, Shore told me that his personal "brand DNA" was "a punk rocker in a pinstripe suit—that's how I understand myself." But when I met him at his stylish loft office in the Chelsea Market, he turned out to be a young British man in khakis and a sweater. "The classical distinctions between personal life, professional life, what I do in my family, how I set up my business, how I plan my career, are breaking down," Shore said. "It's this whole postmodern idea of the script to life just basically being thrown away, and no one quite knows exactly what they're supposed to do in any given situation. . . . If I can't find true north by looking to the corporation that I work for or by looking to the government or the queen, then ultimately you end up with yourself, you have to find your own truth."

In the 1950s, the organization man was told to find what the marketplace wanted and supply it. But in a talent economy, Shore says, "it's the other way around: Find out what you are, then go look for the space in the marketplace that needs that."

Successful brands must be authentic because "the marketplace smells a rat," and consumers, in deciding whom to trust, are suspicious of any gaps between the image of the person or product being marketed and the underlying reality. "In the old days, somebody would look at a business card and say, 'Oh, this guy's a vice president; I'll put him on a hierarchy.' Now they look at your haircut and your shirt and a box of other stuff, and they say, 'This is the box this guy fits in.' And if what he's doing is not real, if he's only trying to protect an image, they notice."

This leads to the phenomenon of marketed authenticity. "Because consumers are sensitive to inauthenticity, you have to look inside out, not outside in: You have to start from the core and then move outward," Shore said. Only those whose public and private reality are aligned can sustain the attention of the marketplace. Far from trying to capture the authentic self in all of its complexities, however, branding is a technology for the simplification of identity, a response to the short attention span of the audience. "In marketing terms, it's always been about 'strip away, strip away,'" Shore emphasized. "People are troubled about thinking about more than one thing at once. If you're trying to project something and you try to be penetrative into people's consciousness, you have to be absolutely simple and to the point about it all—otherwise people can't hold it." In trying to excavate a person's "brand DNA," Shore says that he is suspicious of long lists of abstract characteristics. "It's too complicated; it's too generic. If I said, 'You are an "Individualistic Maverick," that can describe all people. But if I tell you that someone's a 'Modern-Day Robin Hood,' that's pointed.

You'll remember 'Modern-Day Robin Hood' for ten years." (A few hours later, when I tried to repeat this slogan to my wife, I had already managed to forget it.)

Although presented in the therapeutic language of self-actualization, personal branding is ultimately a technology for the rigid control of personal identity. And while only a sliver of the population will be literal minded enough to resort to technologies of personal branding, many individuals in the age of the Internet are struggling, with varying degrees of success and self-awareness, to master the rigors of personal-impression management. Corporate brands have brand managers who vigilantly ensure that their trademarked wards are never depicted in ways that clash with their brand attributes: The Pillsbury Doughboy's brand guidelines, for example, specify that the Doughboy must always act as "a helper, a teacher, or a friend." When one ad agency proposed a spot that showed the Doughboy mischievously drinking the last sip of milk, the spot was sternly rejected as being out of character. Along the same lines, the cosmopolitan Mr. Peanut will never be permitted to marry, and Walt Disney was famous for declaring that "Mickey would never do that."[31] As branding techniques are applied to the self, individuals find themselves similarly constrained. Puff Daddy can change his name to P. Diddy to rehabilitate his reputation after being charged with gun possession, but if he suddenly became a born-again Christian, he would violate his brand guidelines, which require him to behave outrageously. Maintaining a successful brand requires a degree of self-discipline rather than unregulated self-exposure.

Personal branding claims to help individuals be distinctive so that they can differentiate themselves from the crowd and become more successful competitors in the marketplace of the self. But in the process of seeking distinctiveness, personal branding is ultimately a recipe for a smothering conformity. Branding confuses distinctiveness and individuality. Products can be differentiated from one another with the techniques of advertising and public relations: Coke gives the impression of being different from Pepsi; new Coke appears different from old Coke. "Advertising flourished," as Boorstin noted, "from the effort to produce apparent distinctions."[32] As mass-produced products became more similar, different brands had to be cultivated in order to produce the illusion of differentiation: The focus on "name brands" made the image rather than the product the center of attention. But the application of branding technologies to the self is based on a category error: Individuals can't distinguish themselves from the crowd by measuring their value to the crowd. All of the private attributes of human individuality change shape when they are turned outward and presented to the public: Eros becomes sex; sin becomes crime; guilt becomes shame. When everything is exposed to the crowd, as John Stuart Mill recognized, individuality is impossible. "As the various social eminences which enabled persons entrenched on them to disregard the opinion of the multitude, gradually become levelled; as the very idea of resisting the will of the public, when it is positively known that they have a will, disappears more and more from the minds of practical politicians; there ceases to be any social support for nonconformity,"[33] Mill lamented. "It is individuality we war against," he concluded, because of the "ascendancy of public opinion in the State."[34]

We can now appreciate with special force the distinction between the individuality praised by Mill and the individualism lamented by Tocqueville, which he defined as the tendency of citizens in a democracy to isolate themselves from one another and to focus obsessively on their own self-interest. Even more than the Victorian era, ours is an age of individualism rather than individuality. The growth of media technologies such as the Internet and television has increased the overwhelming authority of public opinion, as citizens in the Omnipticon find more and more aspects of their personal and public lives observed and evaluated by strangers. These technologies tend to encourage citizens to be self-absorbed, as terrifying images from across the country or across the globe give them an exaggerated sense of personal vulnerability. At the same time, by decreasing the distance between central authorities and individual citizens, these technologies lead people to expect personal protection from national leaders, rather than taking responsibility for their own freedom and security at a local level. The related feelings of personal anxiety and personal helplessness feed on themselves, and the technology now exists to bring about the conformity that Mill most feared.

The personal-branding movement is based on the same fantasy that underlay the Portraits of Grief, which is the fantasy that people can achieve emotional intimacy with strangers. But there is no such thing as public intimacy. Intimacy can be achieved only with those who know us; and strangers cannot know us; they can have only information about us or impressions of us. To offer up personal information that has been taken out of context, in an effort to create the illusion of emotional connection with strangers, requires us to homogenize and standardize the very qualities that made the information personal in the first place. The family members of the 9/11 victims who offered up details of their mourning to the *Times* are not so different from the family members of the victim of a car crash who, moments after the accident, weep on cue for the local news. What is most alarming about these scenes is not the tears but the fact that, even at moments of tragedy, we instinctively look at the camera and talk into the microphone.

The personal-branding phenomenon is a crude attempt to provide regulated forms of self-exposure, to maintain some kind of boundary between the public and private in a world where self-revelation has become a social imperative. And, of course, most citizens will never resort to expert assistance in their efforts to present a coherent face to the world. But living in the Omnipticon, where we are increasingly unsure about who is observing us, individuals will have to worry more about acting consistently in public and private in precisely the way the branding advisers prescribe. In the 1980s, before the proliferation of the Web, the sociologist Joshua Meyrowitz discussed the way the electronic media were changing what he called the "situational geography" of social life.[35] As television made us one large audience to performances that occurred in other places, the old walls that separated backstage areas, where people could let down their hair and rehearse for public performances, from the frontstage areas, where the formal performances occurred, began to collapse. Television made viewers aware of the discrepancy between frontstage and backstage behavior (such as the woman who plays hard to get or the fearful man who acts confident in a reality TV dating show), and it became increasingly hard for people to project different images in public and in private without appearing artificial or inauthentic.

Now that the Internet is allowing strangers to observe us even as we observe them, ordinary citizens have to worry more about being caught off guard, like actors without their wigs. As a form of self-defense, all citizens face the same pressures that confused Laurence Tribe: We will increasingly adopt what Meyrowitz called "middle region" behavior in public: a blend of the formal front stage and informal back stage, with a bias toward self-conscious informality. As private concerns like sexual behavior and depression, anxieties, and doubts become harder to conceal, they have to be integrated into the public performance. The result can create an illusion of familiarity— the crazy heavy metal rock star Ozzy Osbourne looked cuddlier (though still scatological) as MTV cameras recorded every moment of his domestic life for a reality TV show. But the cuddly domesticated Osbourne was less eccentric, and less distinctive, than his onstage persona had led audiences to expect.

Like Boorstin, Meyrowitz worried that conformity and homogeneity would result as the electronic media expanded the middle region at the expense of frontstage and backstage behavior. In addition to blurring the boundaries between political leaders and followers, Meyrowitz predicted, the electronic technologies of exposure would blur the boundaries between the behavior of men and women, as well as children and adults. All of these groups speak and act differently when they are segregated from one another; and once the boundaries that separate the groups began to collapse, each of these groups would begin to act more like the others. Now the democratizing technology of the Internet is fulfilling Meyrowitz's fears: As more personal information about ourselves is available on the Web, private figures are feeling the same pressure that public figures have long experienced to expose details of their personal lives as a form of self-defense; and men, women, and children are blurring into an indistinguishable cacophony of intimate exposure.

To the degree that self-revelation to strangers is a bid for relief from anxiety about identity, however, it may not succeed. Social psychologists who have studied the therapeutic effects of emotional disclosure have discovered a consistent pattern: People who receive positive social support for their emotional disclosures tend to feel better as a result, while those who receive negative responses—from indifference to hostility—feel worse. For example, a nationwide study of psychological responses to 9/11 found that those who sought social support and vented their anxieties without receiving positive reinforcement were more likely to feel greater distress during the six months after the attack than those who engaged in more social coping activities such as giving blood and attending memorial services.[36] This is consistent with studies of Vietnam veterans and survivors of the California firestorms, who actually felt worse after sharing their feelings with strangers who made clear they didn't want to listen. ("Thank you for not sharing your earthquake story," read an especially wounding T-shirt.) Those who shared their pain with unreceptive audiences felt worse than those who didn't talk at all, although those who didn't talk at all did not feel as good as those who shared their pain with receptive audiences. Studies of the benefits of writing as well as talking about emotional experiences confirm the same insight: Emotional disclosure can have therapeutic effects when it helps people to become less isolated and more integrated with social networks, but it can have negative effects when it leads people to vent their feelings in a void, without the support of a receptive audience.³⁷ This suggests that therapeutic venting on the Internet to a faceless audience in an unreciprocated bid for attention and emotional support is unlikely to help, and may well make things worse.

The sociologist Ferdinand Tönnies believed that open communications with others could be achieved only in what he called *Gemeinschaft,* or premodern, pre-urban hierarchical communities, where individuals could reveal themselves to social equals confident that boundaries, like the class structure, would be maintained. By contrast, in modern society, or *Gesellschaft,* Tönnies believed that the instability of class would require people to parcel out their emotions, presenting different parts of themselves in different contexts. Richard Sennett calls the nineteenth-century idea that emotional intimacy can be achieved with strangers an example of "destructive gemeinschaft." "For destructive gemeinschaft to arise," he writes, "people must believe that when they reveal their feelings to each other, they do so in order to form an emotional bond. This bond consists of a collective personality which they build up through mutual revelation. And the seeds of this fantasy of being a community by sharing a collective personality were also planted by the terms of 19th Century culture."³⁸ Sennett's principle of destructive gemeinschaft reminds us that although the search for authenticity poses as a form of individual self-expression, it is ultimately a bid for the effacement of individuals into the emotional demands of the crowd. The excesses of individualism can lead, once again, to the destruction of individuality.

The quest for intimacy with strangers in the Naked Crowd, in short, is both compulsive and fraught with peril. The imperative of intimacy comes from the increasing importance of what Anthony Giddens has called the "pure relationship"—a marriage or friendship or intimate partnership where the partners trust each other completely and can guide each other wisely through the bewildering array of choices and pitfalls that individuals in the Naked Crowd face each day in an attempt to sustain a coherent public face. To have found a pure relationship is such a completing experience—a source of such joy and fulfillment—that one hardly imagines how it had been possible to live without it. "To those who cannot conceive it," as Mill writes, "it would appear the dream of an enthusiast."[39] But because personal affinity is a form of alchemy, finding a pure relationship is as difficult as it is necessary; the search itself is hardest of all, and the urge to settle in the face of loneliness can be overwhelming. Without a pure relationship, the anxieties and uncertainties inherent in trying to navigate the shoals of the Naked Crowd can become so unsettling that one imposes them on anyone who will listen—on friends and family members, ideally, but if these are unavailable, on strangers as well. But this fraught and unsatisfying quest for psychological support in the context of publicity rather than intimacy is unlikely to succeed.

The emotional intimacy inherent in a pure relationship can be achieved only in the context of privacy: Without the confidence that our backstage anxieties and confusions won't be revealed to strangers, we can't build the trust necessary to achieve intimacy in the first place, nor the unwavering and reciprocated attention that privacy allows. "Privacy makes possible the psychic satisfactions that the achievement of intimacy has to offer," Giddens recognizes.[40] And even within a pure relationship, couples can't sustain genuine intimacy without having zones of physical and mental privacy to which both people can retreat with their own thoughts. "If ever a man and his wife . . . who pass nights as well as days together, absolutely lay aside all good-breeding," wrote Lord Chesterfield, "their intimacy will soon degenerate into a coarse familiarity, infallibly productive of contempt or disgust. The best of us have our bad sides; and it is as imprudent as it is ill-bred to exhibit them."[41] Even in our own unbuttoned age, human beings need privacy not only in public but in private as well.

In *The Book of Laughter and Forgetting,* Milan Kundera examines the phenomenon of graphomania—the pathological desire to express yourself in writing before a public of unknown readers. "General isolation breeds graphomania, and generalized graphomania in turn intensifies and worsens isolation," Kundera writes. "[E]veryone [is] surrounded by his own words as by a wall of mirrors, which allows no voice to filter through from outside."[42] Kundera contrasts the reticence of his heroine, who is mortified by the idea that anyone except for her beloved might read her love letters, with the graphomania of a writer like Goethe, who is convinced that his worth as a human being will be called into question if a single human being fails to read his words. The difference between the lover and Goethe, he says "is the difference between a human being and a writer."[43] In an indifferent and socially atomized universe, "everyone is pained by the thought of disappearing, unheard and unseen"; as a result, everyone is tempted to become a writer, turning himself "into a universe of words." But "when everyone wakes up as a writer," Kundera warns, "the age of universal deafness and incomprehension will have arrived."[44] Now, we are living in an age of graphomania; we are experiencing the constant din of intimate typing—in e-mail, in chat rooms, in blogs, and in the workplace. The clacking noise we hear in the air is the noise of endless personal disclosure. But, as Kundera recognized, instead of forging emotional connections with strangers, personal exposure in a vacuum may increase social isolation rather than alleviate it.

The crowd wants what it wants, and one thing that it wants is personal exposure from anyone on whom it fixes its irresistible gaze. We have seen the many factors that put tremendous pressure on individuals in the Naked Crowd to expose personal details of their lives and to strip themselves bare. The crowd demands exposure out of a combination of voyeurism, desire for emotional connection, fear of strangers, democratic suspicion of reticence as a sign of elitism, a need for markers of trustworthiness, and an unwillingness to conceive of public events or to relate to public figures except in personal terms. From the perspective of the individual who is pursuing the attention of the crowd, there is, as Charles Derber has suggested, the hope of gaining a mass audience by self-exposure; the demands of a therapeutic culture that rewards people who talk about their intimate problems and cast themselves as victims and survivors; the narcissism that leads people obsessively to call attention to their own fears and insecurities in a world where identity is always up for grabs; and the expansion of democratic technologies that create so many new opportunities for individuals to expose themselves before the crowd.[45] Above all, there is the desire to establish ourselves as trustworthy in a risk society by proving, through exposure, that we have nothing to hide.

All this suggests little cause for optimism that, in the face of future terrorist threats, the crowd will strike the balance between personal security and personal exposure in a reasonable way. Individuals, as we've seen, don't care much about privacy in the aggregate at all: Faced with a choice between privacy and exposure, many people would rather be exposed than be private, because the crowd demands no less. Concerned mainly about controlling the conditions of their own exposure, many people are only too happy to reveal themselves promiscuously if they have the illusion of control. Anxious exhibitionists, trained from the cradle to believe that there is no more valuable currency than public attention, are not likely to object when their neighbors demand that they strip themselves bare. But just as public intimacy is a kind of delusion, so is the hope of distinguishing ourselves from the crowd by catering to the crowd's insatiable demands for exposure. It is impossible to achieve genuine distinction without a certain heedlessness of public opinion. We can turn ourselves into portraits of grief only at the cost of looking more like one another. As both spectators and actors in the Naked Crowd, we are too willing to surrender privacy for an illusory sense of emotional connection and security. Perhaps we will realize what a poor bargain we have struck only after it is too late.

An Escape from Fear

BY THE TIME YOU READ THIS, NORTH AMERICA AND Europe may have been shaken by new waves of terrorist attacks. In the aftermath of the traumatic events, nothing in this book offers any reason to expect that the public will demand laws and technologies that protect liberty and security at the same time. On the contrary, everything we know about the vulnerabilities of the Naked Crowd suggests that new fears will be accompanied by new claims that everything has changed and that we can no longer afford to defend the American values—such as privacy and freedom—that we had taken for granted in calmer times. Refusing to evaluate whether or not these new laws and technologies in fact increase security, the public may willingly acquiesce in the destruction of privacy without getting anything tangible in return. Even if the actual threats are limited and contained, the fears they engender may be exaggerated and corrosive. It's not hard to imagine a mentality of permanent crisis on the part of the public, leading to the steady encroachment of technologies of surveillance and profiling that have no discernible impact in preventing terrorism. And the ineffectiveness of the technologies, perhaps, will provoke further calls for their proliferation.

In light of what we know about the psychology of the Naked Crowd, this scenario may materialize; perhaps it is more likely than not to do so. But each of the relevant actors—the technologists, the lawmakers, the courts, and the public—might be persuaded to strike a more reasonable balance between liberty and security if each were addressed in terms they could understand and accept. In this epilogue, I'd like to review a range of more optimistic scenarios that could save America and other Western democracies from the paralyzing fear that is our greatest enemy. In particular, I'd like to evaluate four different models for protecting liberty and security: the transparency model, the control-use model, the judicial-oversight model, and the political-oversight model. Although each has proved useful in different democracies at different times, I want to argue that political oversight provides the most promising path for America in the twenty-first century.

The transparency model is associated with the author David Brin. In *The Transparent Society,* Brin argues that the proliferation of cameras and surveillance devices is inevitable, unstoppable, and largely beneficial. Instead of trying in vain to resist the spread of cameras and databases with ineffective laws and regulations, Brin insists, we should focus instead on ensuring that everyone can view one another's cameras so that "average citizens share, along with the mighty, the right to access these universal monitors."[1] Brin imagines the wonderful benefits of a metropolis in which every citizen can "use his or her wristwatch television to call up images from any camera in town."[2] In the middle of the night, he enthuses, pedestrians could dial up street cameras to ensure that assailants aren't lurking around the corner; and suitors who are running late can peer benignly at restaurants across town to make sure that their dates haven't left in a huff. Brin insists that police officers will act more responsibly in arresting criminals if they are sure that citizens are scrutinizing their conduct at all times. The danger, he says, isn't that surveillance technology will be used by too many people but by too few. He sings the praises of "wearables"—tiny computers that combine the attributes of a portable camcorder, cell phone, laptop, and pager, and have been used by small bands of "sousveillance" activists in San Francisco and Los Angeles to film the public activities of shopkeepers, ordinary citizens, and the police. He doesn't quail at the idea that the government might dispatch tiny gnat cameras to swarm through the air and spy on citizens, because he is confident that citizens can develop anti-gnat cameras to expose the robotic intruders and force the government to obtain warrants instead.[3] He embraces the possibility of profiling citizens on the basis of their proclivities and behavior, suggesting that a "glass house" effect can protect us from the worst abuses. He praises the benefits of a national ID card and integrated databases, but insists that citizens should demand new levels of "transparency, accountability and outright nakedness on the part of government officials" in exchange. "Create a true inspector general of the United States," he told me. "Draft citizen juries with the power to walk in through any door and badger even the CIA director with questions. Rename the White House the Glass House. Each time the government has asked for new powers, we've said, 'Fine. Show me yours first. Strip.'"

Brin is an engaging provocateur, and he usefully calls our attention to the ways that technologies of transparency can promote democratic accountability. Many surveillance technologies that seem to threaten liberty and privacy when the government refuses to make them transparent seem more reasonable when citizens can confirm that they are being deployed in precisely the ways that the government promises. Consider the example of the e-mail search program formerly known as Carnivore. (Like TIA and CAPPS, it was quickly renamed with a cuddlier acronym, DSC1000.) Carnivore is a search engine that allows the government, when it is searching for a particular e-mail, to sift through all of the messages that have been sent and received by a particular Internet service provider. When the search engine finds the suspicious message, it sets off an alert. If Carnivore operates in the way the government suggests, it might be viewed as a perfectly reasonable search, along the model of the Blob Machine, since it focuses with laserlike precision on guilty information and reveals no innocent information to any human being. By contrast, if Carnivore were seized by rogue government agents, it might be deployed to sift through innocent as well as suspicious e-mail messages, which would look more like the kind of fishing expedition that the framers of the Fourth Amendment meant to prohibit. The way for independent third parties to ensure that Carnivore is being operated reasonably, rather than unreasonably, is for the government to reveal the source code for Carnivore. But the government has refused to reveal the source code, claiming unconvincingly that it would compromise the security of the system. By emphasizing the importance of open sourcing for surveillance technologies in general, Brin reminds us that transparency may help to promote liberty without threatening security.

But although Brin usefully emphasizes the importance of technologies of accountability, he exaggerates the benefits of living in a transparent society and seriously underestimates the costs. On the benefits side, he uncritically cites studies from two British cities—Glasgow and King's Lynn—purporting to show a connection between the installation of CCTV cameras and a drop in crime.[4] Both studies were excluded as methodologically unreliable by the British Home Office's comprehensive review of the empirical evidence about the effectiveness of CCTV, on the grounds that they did not include crime data for control areas.[5] The Home Office's comprehensive review, as I mentioned in chapter 1, found no convincing evidence of a connection between the spread of CCTV and the decline of violent crime, and a negligible effect on crime in public transportation systems and city centers. Throughout Brin's book, one finds similar technopositivistic enthusiasm about the possibility of security benefits for surveillance technologies without a careful evaluation of the empirical evidence.

At the same time, Brin is far too glib about the costs of living in a transparent society. "In the twenty-first century, we have to follow the advice of the journalist who said: 'Live your life as if today's mistake may wind up on page twenty-three,' " he told me. "In such a world, we're all going to have to become more tolerant of each other's small mistakes and to try harder not to make big ones." But Brin is too optimistic about "our" ability to tolerate the mistakes of those we have never met, and his optimism is based on the conflation of information with knowledge. Neighbors in a small town can (sometimes) tolerate one another's weaknesses because they know one another whole and in context. The same neighbor who sees you tipsy every day at noon may also see you being kind to children. By contrast, those who have never met one another face-to-face can have information about one another, but they can never really know one another. As a result, in a world of short attention spans, small mistakes come to define people rather than being a basis for tolerance and understanding.

Brin concludes his book with a sunny vision of the Omnipticon as a global village, with kindly citizens looking over the shoulders of their virtual neighbors to ensure the mutual safety of all. "Busybodies will gossip but you'll know *their* secrets—and you'll be able to leave your doors unlocked. Your bedroom will be protected from snoops by electronic guardians, but most of all by the fact that voyeurs and snoops will fear being caught. . . . Better to know our neighbors (in their multitudes) than to live a fiction of splendid, lonely isolation."[6]

Brin's vision is romantic but unconvincing. True knowledge takes place over time: It is a gradual process of mutual revelation. "Real friendship is a slow grower; and never thrives, unless ingrafted upon a stock of known and reciprocal merit,"[7] wrote Lord Chesterfield. But we can't possibly take the time to know and be known by millions of virtual neighbors whom we will never meet. We can reveal only snippets of ourselves and can have access only to snippets of others, and we risk constantly being judged out of context and confusing the part for the whole. When surveillance technologies that judge people out of context are deployed by government rather than by fellow citizens, furthermore, the dangers of mistaken identification become far more acute. If wrongly identified by a digital database or profiling system, people can lose jobs, be denied health insurance and access to airports, or be vunerable to arrest or blackmail. And although Brin is optimistic about the possibility that citizens might choose technologies like the Blob Machine that protect security while also protecting privacy, he is ultimately too much of a populist to think in a cool-eyed fashion about how to promote the adoption of these technologies if citizens prove indifferent to them. "We may vote as people to tell the watchers: 'Make your cameras just acute enough to catch the bad guys,' " he told me. But he has nothing to say about what happens when we vote to install cameras that inhibit the innocent without catching the guilty. For this reason, it seems useful to remember Brin's lessons about the virtues of transparency in government while resisting his enthusiasm about the virtues of living in glass houses.

The second model for protecting liberty and security might be called the control-use model. One of its advocates, William Stuntz, argues that the executive branch should be given expanded surveillance authority but only if it is prohibited from using any evidence that the surveillance reveals to prosecute low-level crimes, as opposed to murder or terrorism. Stuntz's insight is powerful, and he reminds us of the dangerous possibility that general data searches, justified in the name of fighting serious crimes, may quickly become excuses for fishing expeditions that yield evidence of relatively trivial crimes. But there are obvious objections to the control-use model. Many citizens see nothing wrong with using broad surveillance authority to collect evidence of trivial as well as serious crimes. And as the prosecution of Al Capone demonstrated, there are clearly benefits to using convictions for low-level crimes, such as tax evasion, to imprison suspects when the police know they have committed far more dangerous crimes, but can't quite prove the more serious charges. Before and after 9/11, federal officials have used versions of the Al Capone strategy to prosecute those whom they have suspected as terrorists without having proof beyond a reasonable doubt.

In a case from 1991, for example, the State of Missouri charged Zein Hassan Isa, a naturalized U.S. citizen born in Palestine, with the murder of his daughter. Isa had been targeted as a suspected agent of the Palestine Liberation Organization, and the government obtained a foreign intelligence surveillance warrant to tap his home. While he was being covertly tapped, Isa became enraged at finding his daughter at home with a boyfriend, a lapse of virtue that he claimed dishonored his family. Within earshot of the microphones, he took a knife and stabbed her to death. "Quiet, little one!" he exclaimed in Arabic as his wife held the daughter down by the hair. "Die quickly, my daughter, die!"[8] When the State of Missouri tried to introduce the foreign intelligence surveillance tapes as part of Isa's prosecution for murder, Isa objected that his Fourth Amendment rights had been violated on the grounds that the tapes concerned a "private domestic matter" that was not relevant to the foreign intelligence investigation that had authorized the original wiretap. But a federal court rejected his argument, noting that the Foreign Intelligence Surveillance Act allows the retention and sharing of information that is "evidence of a crime" and contains no requirement that the crime be related to foreign intelligence.[9] The court noted other cases where suspected agents of foreign powers had been indicted for credit card fraud.[10] Therefore, the court refused to suppress the evidence.

The court's conclusion seems correct on several levels: Murder is too serious a crime to overlook, and the Foreign Intelligence Surveillance Court had already found probable cause to believe that Isa was an agent of a foreign power; for this reason, indicting him for a crime not directly related to terrorism might have helped to prevent him from committing acts of terror. (There was also a dispute about whether he had killed the daughter to conceal his terrorist plans.) The Foreign Intelligence Surveillance Court of Review made a similar argument in upholding the Bush administration's effort to tear down the rigid wall that separates foreign intelligence surveillance from criminal prosecution. In efforts to prevent terrorism, the court recognized, criminal prosecution and intelligence gathering may converge: Arresting and prosecuting terrorists may be the best way of preventing them from carrying out their violent schemes.[11] Similarly, ordinary crimes may be intertwined with foreign intelligence crimes: As the court noted, if a group of terrorists committed bank robberies to finance the manufacture of bombs, evidence of the bank robbery should be treated as evidence of the terrorist act.[12] For this reason, the court rejected the argument that the government can engage in sweeping foreign intelligence surveillance without a judicial warrant only when its "primary purpose" is intelligence gathering rather than law enforcement, and it also emphasized that the government should be free to prosecute suspected terrorists for lower-level crimes that are discovered in the course of the surveillance. At the same time, the court emphasized that foreign intelligence surveillance shouldn't be used as an excuse to investigate ordinary crimes that are completely unrelated to terrorist acts. When criminal prosecution is the sole purpose of an investigation, therefore, the government must obtain a criminal warrant.

All this suggests that broad forms of what Roger Clarke calls "personal dataveillance" should be permissible when the government has probable cause to believe that a particular individual is especially dangerous. And once the government plausibly believes that an individual is dangerous, it should be able to resort to the Al Capone strategy, prosecuting him or her for lower-level crimes unrelated to terrorism as a way of getting the suspect off the streets. By contrast, when the government engages in "mass dataveillance," without cause to suspect particular individuals of particular crimes, the situation looks very different. If the government were able to use the Al Capone strategy here, and prosecute people for crimes unrelated to terrorism when they posed no special dangers to society at large, many citizens might feel as if they were living in a police state. For this reason, mass dataveillance could be permitted as a tool of risk prediction, as opposed to criminal investigation, only when there are limitations imposed on how the government can use evidence of ordinary crimes unrelated to terrorism. A model here might be the German wiretap law, which allows intelligence authorities to use wiretaps for domestic surveillance only when there is factual basis to suspect that one of a list of crimes involving a threat to national security has been, or is about to be, committed. The German law says that evidence obtained through wiretapping can be used only in the investigation and prosecution of specified national security crimes or certain other serious crimes; if the intelligence officers find evidence of low-level crimes, they may not share it with law enforcement officers or introduce it in court.[13] Although legal limitations on the use of evidence obtained by mass dataveillance are worth exploring, they may be difficult to sustain in practice for the reasons I discussed in chapter 3: In America, the political pressure to expand the list of crimes for which wiretaps could be justified has proved too overwhelming to resist.

A third model for protecting liberty and security focuses on judicial oversight. I've argued that it would be foolish to expect that judges will (or should) take positions about privacy that vary dramatically from what the public demands. Conceptions of what kinds of searches are reasonable and unreasonable under the Constitution depend crucially on public conceptions of reasonableness, and because judges have shown little willingness to cast themselves as crusaders for privacy in the past, there is little reason to count on them to pave the way in the immediate future.

Over the long term, it's possible that some kind of constitutional restraints on dataveillance and electronic monitoring of citizens might evolve. Social changes, after all, move slowly through the courts: Nearly two decades elapsed between the time that the California Supreme Court first invalidated an antimiscegenation law in 1948 and the time the Supreme Court struck down all state laws prohibiting interracial marriage in 1967.[14] (It took Alabama voters another three decades before they repealed the last such law in 2000.)[15] Along the same lines, it took the Supreme Court nearly forty years from 1928, when it held that wiretapping wasn't a search because it didn't involve a physical trespass, to 1967, when it changed its mind and held that wiretapping was an unreasonable search because the Fourth Amendment protects "people, not places."[16] Although the transformation may be similarly slow in coming, it's not impossible to imagine that the Supreme Court might gradually abandon its circular focus on subjective expectations of privacy and come to recognize, as Justice Harlan did, that the analysis of unreasonable searches in an electronic age must "transcend the search for subjective expectations or legal attributions of assumption of risk."[17] In Harlan's view, the question of whether a particular search is unreasonable must be answered "by assessing the nature of a particular practice and the likely extent of its impact on the individual's sense of security balanced against the utility of the conduct as a technique of law enforcement." He concluded that "[t]he impact of the practice of third-party bugging must, I think, be considered such as to undermine that confidence and sense of security in dealing with one another that is characteristic of individual relationships between citizens in a free society."[18]

Harlan was in dissent, and his views have never attracted a Supreme Court majority. But Canada's former privacy commissioner challenged the use of video surveillance on similar grounds, claiming that ubiquitous video monitoring, like hidden microphones, inhibits the spontaneity that can only flourish if individuals are confident that their daily interactions in a free society aren't routinely being recorded or observed. At the privacy commissioner's request, Gérard La Forest, the former justice of the Canadian Supreme Court, wrote an eloquent advisory opinion expressing his own view that generalized surveillance, whether recorded or not, violated "the right to be secure against unreasonable search or seizure" guaranteed by

Section 8 of the Canadian Charter. Mirroring Harlan's reasoning, he insisted that the constitutional test shouldn't be whether a particular surveillance technology is in widespread use, but whether it is "inconsistent with the aims of a free and open society." In his view, dragnet video surveillance in public places could not pass this test, because it was more consistent with a police state than a free society. "We may not have a reasonable expectation that the police will *never* observe our activities in public spaces, either incidentally or as part of a targeted investigation," he wrote. "But surely it is reasonable to expect that they will not *always* do so."[19] Unlike surveillance that is targeted at particular suspects, in other words, La Forest concluded that ubiquitous video surveillance in public is unreasonable because it inhibits the innocent and guilty alike.

There is, however, an unsettling element of subjectivity in asking judges to make a value judgment about whether or not a particular surveillance technology is consistent "with the aims of a free and open society."[20] In my view, this inquiry gives courts too much discretion to decide what kind of freedom from surveillance they think an open society requires. In examining a new technology of dataveillance, courts might be persuaded instead to follow the lead suggested by Harlan himself, examining the "extent of its impact on the individual's sense of security balanced against the utility of the conduct as a technique of law enforcement."[21] This cost-benefit analysis could ask the kinds of questions courts have traditionally asked in deciding whether or not to permit a search without a warrant or individualized suspicion, examining the invasiveness of the search, the amount of discretion entrusted to the police officers, the necessity of the search, and its likely effectiveness.

These questions are consistent with the ones that the Supreme Court generally asks in deciding whether to allow searches without warrants, where it has forbidden the use of roadblocks as a means of ordinary crime control but has noted that "the Fourth Amendment would almost certainly permit an appropriately tailored roadblock set up to thwart an imminent terrorist attack or to catch a dangerous criminal who is likely to flee by way of a particular route."[22]

A cost-benefit analysis along these lines might suggest that the most invasive forms of mass dataveillance are unreasonable and ineffective when deployed for general law enforcement purposes rather than being targeted at terrorism. In evaluating the constitutionality of Canada's proposal to create a database of the travel information of airline passengers that would be available to any state agency for any reason, Justice La Forest objected that "information about one's movements and travel activities should not as a general rule be made available to the state without cause," and that when people are forced to reveal information about their movements, they reasonably expect the state not to "record, compile, or maintain this information for general law enforcement purposes."[23] Evidence that general data searches of passenger information have not been effective in identifying terrorists would add weight to the analysis. But in order to perform a well-informed cost-benefit analysis of a particular security technology, the public, courts, and other reviewing bodies would need access to empirical data about its effectiveness, as they currently have access to wiretap reports. In this sense, transparency, privacy, and security are mutually reinforcing.

A difficulty with the cost-benefit analysis suggested by Justices Harlan and La Forest is that it might re-create some of the circularity of the current judicial doctrines for regulating privacy, allowing privacy interests to recede as technology becomes more effective. For this reason, some European countries have given judges a more aggressive role in deciding on behalf of society how much privacy the government may reasonably invade. The German constitution, for example, establishes a principle of proportionality (*Verhältnismässigkeit*) that authorizes German judges to balance, in each case, a defendant's privacy interests against the strength of the suspicion and the seriousness of the offense. Invoking this doctrine, German courts have held that a greater intrusion will not be permitted when a less intrusive method would be sufficient.[24] The German federal constitutional court has invoked the proportionality principle to hold that taking spinal fluid from a suspect to decide whether or not he was insane was disproportionately invasive given the misdemeanor charge he faced.[25] Unlike American courts during the Clinton impeachment, a German court also refused to admit a private diary turned over to the police by the wife of a defendant's paramour in a case involving perjury. Although the diary might have been admitted if it contained evidence of felonies or international espionage, the court held, the gravity of the invasion in this case outweighed the low-level nature of the suspected crime.[26]

Even more ambitiously, Article 8 of the Council of Europe Convention for the Protection of Human Rights and Fundamental Freedoms, an international convention adopted in 1950, declares that "everyone has the right to respect for his private and family life, his home and his correspondence." It goes on to say that "there shall be no interference by a public authority with the exercise of this right except as is in accordance with the law and is necessary in a democratic society in the interests of national security, public safety or the economic well-being of the country, for the prevention of disorder or crime, for the protection of health or morals, or for the protection of the rights and freedoms of others." Article 8 has been interpreted by the European Court of Human Rights to require national legislatures to adopt laws protecting data privacy; the European Court has also used it to require a kind of heightened judicial scrutiny for government actions that invade privacy, authorizing judges to strike down laws and technologies if there are alternatives that are more respectful of privacy and at least as effective in protecting security. The court has held that the main object of Article 8 is to protect the individual against arbitrary actions by public authorities that are out of proportion to the threat at hand;[27] and using these abstract tests, it has held that monitoring and surveillance of people in public as well as private places may invade the sanctity of private life "once any systematic or permanent record comes into existence of such material from the public domain."[28] Invoking the same principle, the court has invalidated listening devices recording the voices of suspects in a police station and in their cells, and it has also ruled against the Romanian Intelligence Service for releasing information about a citizen's political activities that had been collected by the secret police. Because Romanian law provided no safeguards for gathering and archiving personal data about systems, the court concluded that it conferred arbitrary discretion on public authorities.[29]

It's possible to imagine a similar kind of heightened judicial scrutiny for privacy in America, in which American judges could combine the judicial activism that enjoys bipartisan support in cases involving free speech with broad, European-style protections against privacy invasions that are disproportionate to the threats at hand. A judicial doctrine that strictly scrutinized all laws and technologies infringing on privacy might adopt as its model the four-part test proposed by George Radwanski, the former privacy commissioner of Canada, to help courts and legislators evaluate the appropriateness of surveillance proposals. Any such law or technology, he argues, must be (1) demonstrably necessary to address a particular need or problem, (2) likely to be effective in addressing the problem, (3) proportional to the importance of the problem or the expected security benefit, and (4) there must be no less privacy-intrusive way of achieving the same result.[30] In Radwanski's view, the kind of mass dataveillance that is being considered in Canada and the United States can't be justified in light of these four principles because there is little evidence it is effective in predicting terrorist behavior or identifying known terrorists, because its costs to the privacy of innocent citizens far outweigh its security benefits, and because human intelligence would be more effective in keeping terrorists off airplanes. After concluding that a particular technology is unreasonable—that costs to privacy and equality outweigh the benefits to security—judges applying heightened scrutiny might give legislators and technologists a chance to redesign the technology in ways (like the Blob Machine or the Dutch PrivaCam) that strike a better balance. In evaluating invasive surveillance technologies such as wiretapping, courts have required that they be implemented in ways that minimize the detection of private activity unrelated to the objectives of the search. Using privacy-enhancing technologies, it wouldn't be impossible to design data searches and video surveillance that minimized the recording and storage of personally identifiable information.

Although the judicial-oversight model may make sense in other countries, I am not persuaded by it, and I don't believe that American judges will or should cast themselves in the role of saviors in attempting to balance liberty and security. The history of American judicial activism in hotly contested areas where the country is divided and there are strong passions on both sides should be a cautionary tale. The abortion wars are only the most dramatic example of how judges who presume to enforce privacy rights with shadowy support in the text and history of the Constitution may provoke political backlashes that harm the cause of privacy more than they help it. Moreover, the victims of mass dataveillance are not vulnerable or unpopular minority groups, but all citizens whose personal data is unreasonably scanned and exposed to the state. For this reason, privacy advocates should be able to make their case in the political arena, and to the degree that the political branches are unresponsive, their indifference will reflect the zero-risk mentality of public opinion in general rather than prejudice or antipathy to particular groups. The excesses of the crowd are the Achilles' heel of democracy to which there is and should be no judicial remedy.

In my view, the most promising of the four models for protecting liberty and security is the last one, the political-oversight model. This model holds that Congress is better suited than the courts to strike a reasonable balance between liberty and security for many reasons. Judges tend to be reactive and slow moving, meaning that their decisions often lag behind technology, while Congress can pass laws proactively, as it did when it regulated e-mail privacy as early as 1986. Congress can legislate with flexibility and nuance, tailoring its regulations more closely to the particular challenges raised by particular technologies, while judges tend to prefer bright lines and abstract principles. As I argued in chapter 4, the most important advances for privacy regulation since 9/11 have been congressional rather than judicial—from the repudiation of the Total Information Awareness program to the regulation of the Carnivore e-mail surveillance program to the periodic review of the most invasive provisions in the USA Patriot Act.

The great political challenge for the future is how Congress can be persuaded to create oversight mechanisms that protect liberty and security in a thoughtful way. One model, more in the European than the American tradition, is the Office of the Privacy Commissioner of Canada, which has been a vigorous advocate for the enforcement of privacy laws. The office was created by the Canadian Parliament in the 1980s to defend fair information practices; and the commissioner today has broad and independent powers to investigate privacy complaints, to conduct audits on state agencies, and to refer cases to court. After 9/11, George Radwanski, the former privacy commissioner, criticized the Canadian government's proposals for dataveillance on a broad scale. In particular, the government proposed to require commercial air carriers to provide passenger information to the Canadian Security Intelligence Service and the police, creating a database that could then be searched not only to find suspected terrorists but also to identify anybody wanted on any warrant for any offense punishable by five years or more in jail. Radwanski argued that the database might be justified if passenger information was used only to stop terrorist activity before it occurs. But the same intrusion was unacceptable, he insisted, when the information was used to search for ordinary criminals and to force all travelers to identify themselves to the police.[31] Radwanski also criticized a related proposal—similar to the CAPPS II profiling system being developed in the United States—that would give the Canadian customs agency the authority to collect passenger information on every air traveler entering Canada. The information would include the names, citizenship, and nationality of the travelers; their flights and destinations; their travel documents; and the form of payment. The Canadian intelligence agency has announced that it will retain the information in an extensive national database for six years, and that the database will be accessible to other government agencies not only for fighting terrorism but also for tracking pedophiles, money launderers, tax evaders, and perhaps even frequent travelers to Thailand.[32] As in the United States, the Canadian customs agency plans to perform intelligence analysis on the passenger information to identify behavior patterns that might anticipate future threats, and also to use the database to solve crimes after they have occurred.

Given the relative success of the office of the Canadian privacy commissioner in acting as a public advocate for privacy, a similar office might, in theory, help to balance liberty and security in the United States. Privacy advocates have long sought such an office, ever since the Senate recommended the creation of a federal privacy commission in 1974, but the proposal was tabled thanks to opposition by the Ford administration. "I do not favor the establishment of a separate Commission or broad bureaucracy empowered to define privacy in its own terms and to second-guess citizens and agencies," Ford declared.[33] As Ford's statement suggests, Americans are more suspicious than Canadians of expert administrative bodies, which they perceive to be elitist and bureaucratic. Canada, by contrast, has been described as a "pleasantly authoritarian" culture, with far greater trust in government and willingness to defer to experts. Nevertheless, if Congress delegated the functions of a privacy agency to a special oversight committee, rather than to a broad new bureaucracy, some of the libertarian concerns of those who are worried about privacy but are suspicious of government might be mollified.

Conceptions of privacy, liberty, and equality vary dramatically among different Western democracies, and each country's legislative response to the challenge of balancing liberty and security should reflect its unique political culture. A distinctively American response, therefore, might emphasize the importance of congressional resistance to the executive's attempts to expand its own power. As Marc Rotenberg of the Electronic Privacy Information Center has argued, one way to understand the challenge of balancing liberty and security after 9/11 is to consider the model of checks and balances in the U.S. Constitution. That means that if Congress grants the president new authority to engage in foreign intelligence surveillance, it should also create new means of congressional oversight, or if the Office of Homeland Security proposes a trusted traveler program, it should be subject to open government standards.

Rather than creating a new federal agency, in the model of the Environmental Protection Agency or the Food and Drug Administration, Congress could authorize an existing congressional committee to review the effectiveness of new surveillance methods, balancing their costs to privacy against their benefits to security, and making recommendations about whether or not they are justified. The oversight committee could also collect data about the effectiveness of particular architectures of data mining and profiling, which it could compare with data about the effectiveness of the best available alternatives. Although Congress hasn't yet been moved to impose this kind of oversight, for the reasons I discussed in chapter 4, there is a long tradition in America of legislative checks on new forms of surveillance and, over time, meaningful oversight is more likely to come from Congress than the courts.

The attempt by privacy groups to seek political accountability through transparency and coalition building strikes me as the most promising way of balancing liberty and security in the American political system. But the liberties threatened by dataveillance and other security technologies should not be defined exclusively in terms of privacy. In a comprehensive survey of federal laws protecting privacy, published in the 1990s, Priscilla Regan found that communications, information, and workplace privacy issues were on Congress's agenda for years, or even decades, before legislation finally emerged. "In these three cases, the initial policy issue was defined as one of 'privacy,'" she wrote. "But in each case, protecting privacy involved costs to fairly defined interests—government agencies, law enforcement and intelligence officials and employers. These interests were therefore concerned about redefining the issue from the idea of privacy to another idea, such as efficiency, crime control, or honesty and productivity in the workplace."[34] Regan concluded that "privacy as an idea has not had a powerful influence on policy making,"[35] because its abstract and amorphous nature makes it easy for more concrete interests to capture the attention of Congress: When presented with a choice between privacy in general and a more specific value, like crime control, Congress has tended to choose security.

Also, by framing the policy debates in terms of individual rights—in particular, the right of individuals to control information about themselves—policy advocates have invited a focus on cloying personal anecdotes of privacy victims who can make the case that their own privacy has been violated. Members of the public tend to perceive these stories as the missteps of a few unlucky bumblers and aren't convinced that they might suffer a similar fate. When individuals conclude that they themselves are not immediately at risk, they are perfectly happy to sacrifice privacy in the long term for an (illusory) promise of security in the short term.[36] Regan found that when the legislative debates were redefined as a battle that pitched security against more specific interests than privacy, Congress was willing to strike a reasonable balance. "In the case of information privacy, fair information principles replaced privacy in policy discourse; in communication privacy, industry competitiveness replaced privacy; and in psychological privacy, employment opportunities replaced privacy,"[37] Regan concluded. Once privacy advocates made alliances with other groups who could make the case for legislation in terms of the public good, rather than individual rights, they were more successful. Thus, when it came to protecting e-mail privacy in 1986, industry groups were persuaded to rally around the bill after they came to believe that their own business interests were at stake.

If history is any guide, therefore, the most effective way of persuading Congress to strike a reasonable balance between liberty and security is not to focus exclusively on the ways that dataveillance threatens privacy. Instead, Congress might also be urged to focus on the threat to less amorphous and more empirically measurable values, such as equality. I've argued throughout this book that dataveillance threatens to make it harder for individuals to redefine themselves; it is a technology of classification and exclusion that attempts to put people in different boxes, predicting their behavior in the future based on their behavior in the past. In this sense, it changes not merely the way that citizens relate to one another as individuals but the way that the state relates to them as a group: Instead of treating all citizens as presumptively equal, the government is now treating some as more trustworthy and valuable than others. After groups of individuals are routinely discriminated against at airports, in applying for jobs, or in trying to enter federal buildings, it's not hard to imagine that the resulting uproar (and lawsuits) could galvanize Congress into regulating technologies of dataveillance. But even before particular scandals emerge, the language of equality may have enough political resonance to form the basis of an effective and broad-based coalition for reform.

Political oversight seems more promising in America than judicial fiat; but in any democracy, the future of the balance between liberty and security will depend crucially on the attitudes of the public itself. This has been a book about the vulnerabilities of the Naked Crowd, and although I've not been optimistic about the ability of the public to make calm judgments about liberty when it feels under siege, the picture is not entirely bleak. There are strong social pressures to embrace ineffective, feel-good technologies of security in the immediate wake of an attack; but the public is often able to reach a more considered judgment after the initial fears have faded, more information becomes available, and a sufficiently vocal minority begins to raise questions about the costs and benefits of the technology in question.

Immediately after 9/11, more than six in ten Americans agreed that the average person would have to give up civil liberties to fight terrorism. By June 2002, however, the number had fallen to 46 percent.[38] Along the same lines, recall the shift in public opinion about national identification cards. A poll conducted the week after the 9/11 attacks found that 70 percent of the respondents supported the idea of a national ID card that would have to be shown to officials on demand. Six months later, however, another poll found that only 26 percent of Americans backed the proposal, while 41 percent opposed it.[39] The shift reflected growing concern that government agencies would use the information for reasons that had nothing to do with terrorism; the public was also moved by the arguments of privacy advocates that the system would be ineffective in identifying determined terrorists, many of whom had obtained valid IDs in the past. The shift in public attitudes toward ID cards is consistent with studies of group psychology that have found that people are less susceptible to group pressure when they have more information about a topic and are therefore more confident about their opinions. In the face of a unified majority, many individuals will take the group's view despite empirical evidence to the contrary. But when vocal minorities present a contrary view, people are more likely to act independently. And as the television pictures of burning buildings faded from memory, so did the demand for unrealistic precautions. This is why it's important to be cautious about constructing, in the heat of passion, vast architectures of surveillance and identification that will linger long after fears have subsided and the immediate danger has passed.

If the public is to have a chance of resisting the temptations of crippling fear, it will have to be addressed in ways that promote trust rather than undermine it. Psychologists of fear have found that the most effective risk communication takes account of the limitations and peculiarities of the public mind. Imagine the dirty bomb scenario that I discussed in chapter 2: How could the relatively low risks of contamination be conveyed to the public in a way that would avoid a mass panic? There is no point in presenting dry statistics about remote risks: Studies of risk communication have found that telling people that the annual risk of living next to a nuclear power plant is equivalent to the risk of riding an extra three miles in a car fails to calm them down, because people have difficulty comparing unrelated risks; they tend to become confused and angry instead.[40] Merely being presented with evidence about the low risk of contamination may have the perverse effect of increasing public fears of being contaminated: When people are briefed about the low risks of radiation exposure from electric and magnetic fields, they tend to become more concerned rather than less, because they remember the scary pictures of radiation rather than the reassuring numbers that accompany them.[41] More effective risk communication tends to compare different forms of radiation risk: When traces of radiation from Chernobyl reached the United States, for example, the EPA noted that exposures in the United States were a tiny fraction of the exposure from chest X rays; and this seemed to reassure U.S. citizens. By contrast, similar comparisons in Europe failed to alleviate high public anxiety that had little relation to the actual threats, because the media and the public didn't trust the sources of information.[42]

By all accounts, trust is the most important factor in avoiding mass panic: The public has to trust the credibility of official sources of information in order to believe them. People accept the risks of X rays and prescription drugs because they trust the medical profession, but they are fearful of nuclear power because they don't trust the managers of nuclear power plants.[43] In order to inspire trust, government officials and media outlets have to convey the facts as accurately as they can, avoid spin, and candidly confess the limits of their knowledge rather than pretending to be more technically competent than they are. Israel has used this model since the 1960s: By and large, citizens trust that the government gives them truthful information, however bad the news is, within the limits of what is possible to convey without compromising the country's security. Unfortunately, in the United States, where citizens are instinctively distrustful of government, this kind of candor is hard to come by: At the height of the anthrax scare, the director of homeland security broke most of these rules of risk communication—speculating on the basis of incomplete knowledge, giving unhelpful risk comparisons to unrelated threats (the risk of being infected by anthrax was less than the risk of auto accidents, he said), and feigning a knowledge of the facts he didn't possess. At the same time, he failed to convey a crucial piece of information: Many people didn't realize that they had to be exposed to anthrax in order to be infected.[44]

In the case of radiological danger, the possibilities of a public backlash against incompetent and dissembling officials are much greater. People have trouble understanding the risks of radiological weapons because of a basic confusion between radiation and radioactivity. A study of people's understanding of the risks of radon in their homes found that the EPA, to its credit, had tried to convey accurate information, but homeowners were confused because they thought, reasonably but incorrectly, that if their house had radon in it, it was permanently contaminated. To disabuse the public of this confusion, the EPA would have had to explain that although a small amount of rapidly decaying radon can do damage, once the influx has been stopped, there is no danger. But because citizens are reluctant to absorb scientific information relating to technologies that they fear, this sort of message would likely be lost in the media din.

I've described a hypothetical set of events that would have to transpire in order to avoid fear and panic in the face of future terrorist attacks. But it's hard to be optimistic that all of these pieces of the puzzle will fall into place. "In a risk society there is a new moral climate of politics, one marked by a push-and-pull between accusations of scaremongering on the one hand and of cover-ups on the other," Anthony Giddens writes. "A good deal of political decision-making is now about managing risks—risks which do not originate in the political sphere, yet have to be politically managed. If anyone—government official, scientific expert or lay person—takes any given risk seriously, he or she must announce it. It must be widely publicized, because people must be persuaded that the risk is real—a fuss must be made about it. However if a fuss is indeed created and the risk turns out to be minimal, those involved will be accused of scaremongering."[45] We saw this dynamic with the color-coded terrorism alerts that the Office of Homeland Security issued to calibrate the threats of violence on a daily basis. During the year after the 9/11 attacks, none of the predicted threats materialized, but the political pressure to show that the government was serious about protecting the public from terrorism remained so great that the alerts continued. As amplified by the cable TV media, they created more fear than they assuaged, and created a kind of public fatigue that made it less likely that the government and the television spokesmen would be trusted when a serious threat finally materialized.

There are many ways that trust is destroyed in a political culture that is skeptical of authority. As Paul Slovic has discussed, the fact that individuals give more weight and attention to negative events means that the media will do so as well: Scientific studies showing increased risk for death and disease get more attention than studies with less gloomy conclusions.[46] Special interest groups have an incentive to use their own experts to sow mistrust among the public in order to influence policy debates. And a general mistrust of government, which can be healthy in checking executive excesses, means that experts of any stripe will be greeted with skepticism. At the end of his study of public opinion, Walter Lippmann called earnestly for the creation of an administrative cadre of experts who would sort through information about science and foreign affairs that was too complicated to be digested by an easily distracted public. Today, a similar proposal would be even less plausible than it was when Lippmann wrote in the 1920s: No expert can command deference by virtue of his or her position;

and even the experts, dependent on the public for status and recognition, have the same incentive to exaggerate risks and pander to public fears as the political branches. All this is to say that even if the executive branch, the media, and the scientific community didn't have their own reasons to fan the public's fears rather than assuaging them, it's hardly clear that when trustworthy figures arise during times of crisis, the public will be inclined to trust them for long.

It should be obvious, by this point, that fear itself is indeed our most intractable enemy—as Roosevelt called it "nameless, unreasoning, unjustified terror which paralyzes needed efforts to convert retreat into advance."[47] We are now experiencing the peculiar weaknesses of a society ruled by public opinion—the narcissistic individualism that is the enemy of individuality; the technological egalitarianism that is at odds with genuine equality; and the unrealistic zero-risk mentality that selfishly demands complete insulation from remote dangers that are, by definition, impossible to eliminate. To overcome the weaknesses of the Naked Crowd, we will have to learn to live with our own anxieties and fears, rather than unrealistically demanding their eradication. And in this regard, our success in overcoming our fears may depend crucially on bold and farseeing political leadership, of the kind that Rudolph Giuliani, the former mayor of New York City, offered in the wake of the 9/11 attacks. The greatest leaders of democracies in earlier wars did not pander to public fears; instead, they challenged citizens to transcend their self-involved anxieties and to embrace ideals of liberty larger than themselves. It is hard to imagine Franklin Roosevelt instituting a color-coded system of terrorist threat levels. The great wartime leaders encouraged citizens to see themselves as part of a larger struggle, rather than encouraging them to focus obsessively on their own vulnerabilities. Without enlightened political leadership that has the courage to challenge the public's emotionalism, rather than encouraging it at every turn, democracies may not find the inner resources to stay calm in the face of an uncertain future.

A model for the kind of leadership we need might, perhaps, be found in Lincoln's address to the Young Men's Lyceum of Springfield, Illinois.[48] In the speech, delivered in 1838, Lincoln argued that the greatest danger facing America came not from some "transatlantic military giant" such as European or Asian or African invaders. If the danger was to reach our shores, Lincoln argued, "it must spring up amongst us; it cannot come from abroad. If destruction be our lot we must ourselves be its author and finisher." The danger that Lincoln feared most was mob rule—"the increasing disregard for law which pervades the country—the growing disposition to substitute the wild and furious passions in lieu of the sober judgment of courts, and the worse than savage mobs for the executive ministers of justice." He noted the wave of mob violence that was sweeping the country from New England to Louisiana—the lynching of gamblers, the burning of slaves, the shooting of newspaper editors, and the execution of suspected murderers. In the midst of a nation seized by the "mobocratic spirit," Lincoln worried that a dictator might rise up among the people, resolved to destroy their constitutional liberties in order to satisfy his own ambition. To fortify against this danger, Lincoln urged his audience to be guided by reason—"cold, calculating, unimpassioned reason"—rather than the passion that "has helped us, but can do so no more." He concluded by challenging his audience to revere the laws and the Constitution in the face of their anxieties and fears. "Let every American, every lover of liberty, every well-wisher to his posterity swear by the blood of the Revolution never to violate in the least particular the laws of the country, and never to tolerate their violation by others." Instead of flattering the crowd, Lincoln challenged the members of his audience to transcend their baser impulses and embrace an ideal larger than themselves, the ideal of constitutional liberty itself.

The threats that menace us today are different, but the means of resisting them are similar; and they must be found within ourselves and in the best aspects of the American character. No Western democracy that confronted terrorism during the last decades of the twentieth century was transformed beyond recognition by the experience; instead, each society became more like itself. Britain chose to wire itself with surveillance cameras and to embrace technologies of classification that took the place of a caste system that had begun to fray. Israel chose to become more fatalistic at the same time that it became more defiant. Germany chose to resurrect the use of informers but continued to place restrictions on the secret police. France relaxed its restrictions on state information gathering but maintained its restrictions on the press that prohibit it from reporting on the private lives of politicians and celebrities. And so forth. Nations do not reinvent themselves in times of stress; they reveal essential aspects of their character.

America, in this regard, faces a choice. We can choose, in the face of anxiety and fear, to express the weaknesses of the American self—the hyperindividualism that is the enemy of individuality and the crude egalitarianism that is the enemy of equality. We can demand unrealistic levels of personal insurance against remote risks and blame the national government when catastrophes nevertheless arise. Or we can make a different choice. Americans were not always afraid of risk and reluctant to take responsibility for their own fate. The pioneers who settled the open frontier embraced external threats as challenges to be overcome rather than injustices to be litigated. Above all, they were pragmatists, and insisted on empirical evidence before choosing one technology of security or another. They did not embrace snake oil simply because it made them feel safe; instead, they preferred to be safe.

These strengths of the American character—pragmatism, courage, individuality, and self-possession—can be tapped today as readily as our weaknesses. We have it within our power to overcome the paralyzing fears that threaten our liberties. The supreme question that faces us is whether we are ready and willing to save ourselves, rather than demanding salvation from judges or technologists or other illusory protectors. We can, in short, strike a decent balance between freedom and security, as long as we are willing to find that balance in ourselves. Are we?

Acknowledgments

This book is an attempt to respond to a challenge posed by my friend and teacher Lawrence Lessig, whose influence and criticisms have been, as always, definitive. It's always a pleasure to work with Jonathan Karp of Random House, who once again provided invaluable support, candid advice, and constructive guidance from beginning to end. Tim Bartlett of Oxford University Press suggested that I write about liberty and security at a time when I thought I was writing about another topic; uncorked by this suggestion, the argument soon emerged. Chapters 1 and 3 expand on essays that first appeared in *The New York Times Magazine,* and I'm indebted to Adam Moss, Gerry Marzorati, Paul Tough, and James Ryerson for ideal editorial experiences. At *The New Republic,* Martin Peretz, Peter Beinart, and Leon Wieseltier have offered a vibrant home for more than a decade. I'm grateful to Dean Michael Young and my colleagues at the George Washington University Law School for providing the privacy and freedom that makes writing possible, as well as for criticisms of the manuscript that emerged at a faculty Works in Progress workshop. In 2001 and 2002, students in my privacy and security seminar contributed astute ideas and suggestions. Neal Katyal, Lawrence Lessig, Cass Sunstein, Christine Rosen, Marc Rotenberg, Eugene Volokh, and Benjamin

Wittes read the manuscript and generously improved the arguments, especially those with which they disagreed. Lydia Wills was a dedicated agent and Elise Schwartz, Ken Kilgour, and Murray Scheel were wonderful research assistants. I'm very grateful for their help.

Notes

Prologue: The Naked Crowd

1. Kevin Maney, "The Naked Truth About a Possible Airport Screening Device," *USA Today,* August 7, 2002, p. 3B.
2. Mick Hamer, "All-Seeing Scan Spares Your Blushes," *New Scientist,* August 17, 2002, p. 10.
3. Brandon C. Welsh and David P. Farrington, *Crime Prevention Effects of Closed Circuit Television: A Systematic Review,* Home Office Research Study 252, August 2002, p. 44, available at <http://www.homeoffice.gov.uk/rds/pdfs2/hors252.pdf>.
4. Alan M. Dershowitz, "Why Fear National ID Cards?," *The New York Times,* October 13, 2001, p. A23.
5. Steven Brill, *After: How America Confronted the September 12 Era* (New York: Simon & Schuster, 2003), pp. 614–15.
6. Steven L. Nock, *The Costs of Privacy: Surveillance and Reputation in America* (New York: Aldine de Gruyter, 1993).
7. Anthony Giddens, *Self and Society in the Late Modern Age* (Stanford: Stanford University Press, 1991), p. 3.
8. Ibid., p. 126.
9. Ibid., p. 119.
10. Thomas Mathiesen, "The Viewer Society: Michel Foucault's 'Panopticon' Revisited," 1(2) THEORETICAL CRIMINOLOGY 215, 221 (1997).

11. John Stuart Mill, "On Liberty," in *On Liberty and Other Essays* (New York: Oxford University Press, 1998), pp. 73, 81.

12. Gustave Le Bon, *The Crowd: A Study of the Popular Mind* (New York: Ballantine Books, 1969), p. 31.

13. Ibid., p. 62.

14. Ibid., p. 34.

15. See Richard H. Thaler, *Quasi Rational Economics* (New York: Russell Sage Foundation, 1993).

16. See Herbert A. Simon, "Theories of Bounded Rationality," in *Decision and Organization: A Volume in Honor of Jacob Marschak*, ed. B. McGuire and Roy Radner (Amsterdam: North-Holland Publishing Company, 1972).

17. See, e.g., Gerd Gigerenzer and Peter M. Todd, "Fast and Frugal Heuristics: The Adaptive Toolbox," in *Simple Heuristics That Make Us Smart*, ed. Gerd Gigerenzer et al. (New York: Oxford University Press, 1999).

18. Walter Lippmann, *Public Opinion* (New York: The Free Press, 1965), p. 9.

19. Ibid., p. 19.

20. Ibid., p. 202.

21. Ibid., pp. 110–11.

22. Daniel J. Boorstin, *The Image: A Guide to Pseudo-Events in America* (New York: Atheneum, 1987), p. 57.

23. Cass R. Sunstein, *The Laws of Fear: The Perception of Risk,* 115 HARV. L. REV. 1119, 1128–29 (2002).

24. Richard A. Posner, "The Truth About Our Liberties," *The Responsive Community,* summer 2002, p. 5.

25. Daniel J. Solove, *Digital Dossiers and the Dissipation of Fourth Amendment Privacy,* 75 S. CAL. L. REV. 1083 (2002).

26. Roger Clarke, "Information Technology and Dataveillance," November 1987, available at <http://www.anu.edu.au/people/Roger.Clarke/DV/CACM88.html>.

27. Paul Farhi and Linton Weeks, "A Surprise Ending: With the

Sniper, TV Profilers Missed Their Mark," *The Washington Post,* October 25, 2002, p. C1.

28. Ann Davis, "Far Afield: FBI's Post–Sept. 11 'Watch List' Mutates, Acquires Life of Its Own," *The Wall Street Journal,* November 19, 2002, p. A1.

29. Charles Simonyi, "I Fit the Profile," *Slate,* May 25, 1997, available at <http://slate.msn.com/?id=2058>.

30. David Lyon, *The Electronic Eye: The Rise of Surveillance Society* (Minneapolis: University of Minnesota Press, 1994), p. 197.

31. David Lyon, ed., *Surveillance as Social Sorting: Privacy, Risk, and Digital Discrimination* (London and New York: Routledge, 2002).

32. Edward Wong, "In Airport Security, Think Low Tech," *The New York Times,* September 15, 2002, sec. 4, p. 6.

33. Liam Braber, *Korematsu's Ghost: A Post–Sept. 11 Analysis of Race and National Security,* 47 Vill. L. Rev. 451, 457–58 (2002).

34. *Hearing on Airport Security Before the Subcomm. on Aviation of the House Comm. on Transp. and Infrastructure,* 107th Cong. 64 (2001) (statement of Isaac Yeffett).

35. *Regulations Needed to Ensure Air Safety, Hearing Before the House Gov't Reform Energy Policy Subcomm. of the House Natural Resources Comm.,* 107th Cong. 53 (2001) (statement of Isaac Yeffett).

Chapter One: A Cautionary Tale

1. Brandon C. Welsh and David P. Farrington, *Crime Prevention Effects of Closed Circuit Television: A Systematic Review,* Home Office Research Study 252, August 2002, p. vi, available at <http://www.homeoffice.gov.uk/rds/pdfs2/hors252.pdf>.

2. Clive Norris, Jade Moran, and Gary Armstrong, "Algorithmic Surveillance: The Future of Automated Visual Surveillance," in

Surveillance, Closed Circuit Television, and Social Control, ed. C. Norris, J. Moran, and G. Armstrong (Aldershot, U.K.: Ashgate, 1998), p. 255.

3. Brandon C. Welsh and David P. Farrington, *Crime Prevention Effects of Closed Circuit Television: A Systematic Review,* p. 44.

4. Michael McCahill and Clive Norris, "CCTV in London," *Urbaneye Working Paper No. 6,* June 2002, p. 20, available at <http://www.urbaneye.net>.

5. Gary Gumpert and Susan J. Drucker, *Public Boundaries: Privacy and Surveillance in a Technological World,* 49 COMMUNICATION QUARTERLY 115, 121 (2001) (quoting estimate of Clive Norris).

6. Sarah Lyall, "Day 1 of London's Pay-to-Enter Plan for Cars Goes Smoothly," *The New York Times,* February 18, 2003, p. A2.

7. Clive Norris and Gary Armstrong, *The Maximum Surveillance Society: The Rise of CCTV* (Oxford: Berg, 1999), pp. 15–18.

8. Clive Norris, Jade Moran, and Gary Armstrong, "Algorithmic Surveillance: The Future of Automated Visual Surveillance," p. 262.

9. Lee Gomes, "Face-Recognition Technology Questioned," *The Wall Street Journal,* September 27, 2001, p. B11.

10. Michel Foucault, *Discipline and Punish: The Birth of the Prison,* trans. Alan Sheridan (New York: Vintage Books, 1979), p. 201.

11. Kim Campbell, "Stand Still Too Long and You'll Be Watched," *The Christian Science Monitor,* November 7, 2002, p. 17.

12. Stephen Graham, "Toward the Fifth Utility? On the Extension and Normalisation of Public CCTV," in *Surveillance, Closed Circuit Television, and Social Control,* pp. 106–7.

13. See, e.g., "The CCTV Explosion: Thousands More Spy Cameras in £79M. Drive," *The Daily Mail,* August 22, 2001, p. 25.

14. Brandon C. Welsh and David P. Farrington, *Crime Prevention Effects of Closed Circuit Television: A Systematic Review,* p. 1.

15. Ibid., p. vi.

16. Ibid., p. 42.

17. Ibid.

18. David Lyon, *The Electronic Eye: The Rise of Surveillance Society* (Minneapolis: University of Minnesota Press, 1994), p. 197.

19. George Orwell, "The English People," in *Orwell's England* (London: Penguin, 2001), p. 295.

20. Alan F. Westin, *Privacy and Freedom* (New York: Atheneum, 1967), p. 26.

21. See Mark Boal, "Spycam City," *The Village Voice*, September 30–October 6, 1998, available at <http://www.villagevoice.com /issues/9840/boal.php.html>.

22. David Von Drehle, "Nation Reels as Toll Mounts," *The Washington Post*, September 13, 2001, p. A1.

23. Jess Bravin, "Washington Police to Play 'I Spy,' " *The Wall Street Journal*, February 13, 2002, p. B1.

24. *Privacy vs. Security: Electronic Surveillance in the Nation's Capital: Hearing before the Subcomm. on D.C. of the House Comm. on Gov't Reform*, 107th Cong. (2002) (statement of Rep. Constance A. Morella, Chairwoman, House D.C. Subcommittee).

25. Jess Bravin, "Washington Police to Play 'I Spy,' " p. B1.

26. Christopher Slobogin, *Public Privacy: Camera Surveillance of Public Places and the Right to Anonymity*, 72 Miss. L.J. 1, 277 (2002).

Chapter Two: The Psychology of Fear

1. *The Radiological Accident in Goiânia* (Vienna, Austria: International Atomic Energy Agency, 1988), pp. 1–2.

2. *Risk, Media and Stigma: Understanding Public Challenges to Modern Science and Technology*, eds. James Flynn, Paul Slovic, and Howard Kunreuther (London: Earthscan Publications, 2001), pp. 26–27.

3. Ibid., p. 134.

4. Erving Goffman, *Stigma: Notes on the Management of Spoiled Identity* (New York: Simon & Schuster, 1963), p. 1.

5. Ibid., p. 3.

6. Ibid., p. 4.

7. Alan Wolfe, *Moral Freedom: The Search for Virtue in a World of Choice* (New York: W. W. Norton, 2001), p. 88.

8. Peter N. Stearns, *Battleground of Desire: The Struggle for Self-Control in Modern America* (New York: NYU Press, 1999), p. 325.

9. Paul Rozin, "Technological Stigma: Some Perspectives From the Study of Contagion," in *Risk, Media and Stigma*, pp. 31–35.

10. See <http://www.usps.com/news/2001/press/mailsecurity/allfaq.htm>.

11. Richard Benedetto, "Poll Finds Anthrax Fear but No Panic," *USA Today*, October 23, 2001, p. A4.

12. J. Mozingo, "Poll: Floridians Not Panicked," *The Miami Herald*, October 25, 2001, p. 3B.

13. Tom Pelton, "36% of Americans Wash Up after Handling Mail," *The Baltimore Sun*, December 18, 2001, p. 8A.

14. See generally Thomas A. Glass and Monica Schoch-Spana, "Bioterrorism and the People: How to Vaccinate a City Against Panic," in *Confronting Biological Weapons*, CID, January 15, 2002.

15. See generally *U.S. Postal Service Emergency Preparedness Plan for Protecting Postal Employees and Postal Customers from Exposure to Biohazardous Material and for Ensuring Mail Security against Bioterror Attacks*, March 6, 2002, available at <http://www.usps.com/news/2002/epp/welcome.htm>.

16. Paul Slovic, "Trust, Emotion, Sex, Politics and Science: Surveying the Risk-Assessment Battlefield," in Paul Slovic, *The Perception of Risk* (Sterling, Va.: Earthscan, 2000), p. 396.

17. Ibid., pp. 398–99.

18. Jennifer S. Lerner, Roxana M. Gonzalez, Deborah A. Small, and Baruch Fischoff, *Effects of Fear and Anger on Perceived Risks of Terrorism: A National Field Experiment*, PSYCHOLOGICAL SCIENCE (2002).

19. Paul Slovic, Melissa Finucane, Ellen Peters, and Donald G. MacGregor, "The Affect Heuristic," in *Heuristics and Biases: The Psychology of Intuitive Judgment,* eds. T. Gilovich, D. Griffin, and D. Kahneman (Cambridge: Cambridge University Press, 2002), pp. 397, 400.

20. See Amos Tversky and Daniel Kahneman, *Availability: A Heuristic for Judging Frequency and Probability,* 5 COGNITIVE PSYCHOLOGY 207 (1973).

21. Ibid., p. 107.

22. W. Kip Viscusi, "Alarmist Decisions with Divergent Risk Information," 107 EC. JOURNAL 1657 (1997).

23. Cass Sunstein, *Probability Neglect: Emotions, Worst Cases, and Law,* 112 YALE L.J. 61 (2002).

24. Alexis de Tocqueville, *Democracy in America,* eds. Harvey C. Mansfield and Delba Winthrop, vol. 2, part 1, ch. 18 (Chicago: University of Chicago Press, 2000), p. 464.

25. Joel Best, *Random Violence: How We Talk about New Crimes and New Victims* (Berkeley: University of California Press, 1999), p. 10.

26. George Gerbner, "Violence and Terror in and by the Media," in *Media, Crisis and Democracy,* eds. M. Raboy and B. Dagenais (Newbury Park, Calif.: Sage, 1992), pp. 94–107.

27. See, e.g., Bill Keller, "Nuclear Nightmares," *The New York Times Magazine,* May 26, 2002, p. 22; and Gregg Easterbrook, "Why Nukes Are the Only Weapons of Mass Destruction," *The New Republic,* October 7, 2002, p. 22.

28. Roxane Cohen Silver, E. Alison Holman, Daniel N. McIntosh, Michael Poulin, and Virginia Gil-Rivas, *Nationwide Longitudinal Study of Psychological Responses to September 11,* 288 JAMA 1235 (2002).

29. See "Florida Commission Bans Shark Feeding," September 7, 2001, available at <http://www.cnn.com/2001/TRAVEL/NEWS/11/01/shark.feeding.ap/index.html>; see also Cass Sunstein, *Probability Neglect,* 112 YALE L.J. at 100–01 and n. 210.

30. Dale Russkoff, "The Power of Grief," *The Washington Post,* June 22, 1998, p. 27.

31. Philip Hilts, "AMA Urges Full Availability of Breast Implants," *The New York Times,* December 1, 1993, p. A20; see generally Barry Glasser, *The Culture of Fear* (New York: Basic Books, 1999), pp. 164–65.

32. See Smith v. Doe, 123 S. Ct. 1140 (2003) ; see also, Conn. Dep't of Pub. Safety v. Doe, 123 S. Ct. 1160 (2003).

33. "Knife Slips Past Dulles Checkpoint," *The Washington Post,* June 30, 2002, p. C9.

34. Lawrence M. Friedman, *Total Justice* (New York: Russell Sage Foundation, 1994), p. 49.

35. Ibid., p. 43.

36. Paul Slovic, "Perceived Risk, Trust and Democracy," in Paul Slovic, *The Perception of Risk,* p. 317.

37. Ibid., p. 323.

38. Paul Slovic, James Flynn, C. K. Mertz, Marc Poumadere, and Claire Mays, "Nuclear Power and the Public: A Comparative Study of Risk Perception in France and the United States," in *Cross-Cultural Risk Perception: A Survey of Empirical Studies,* eds. O. Renn and B. Rohrmann (Dordrecht, The Netherlands: Kluwer Academic, 2000), p. 98.

39. Bill Durodié, "The Demoralization of Science," pp. 5–6, paper for the Demoralization: Morality, Authority and Power Conference, Cardiff, U.K., 2002, available at <www.cf.ac.uk/socsi/news/dmap/papers/Durodie.pdf>.

40. Ibid., p. 7.

41. Douglas Powell, "Mad Cow Disease and the Stigmatization of British Beef," in *Risk, Media and Stigma,* ed. James Flynn, Paul Slovic, and Howard Kunreuther, p. 222.

42. Ibid.

43. Bill Durodié, "The Demoralization of Science," p. 7.

44. Ibid., p. 8.

45. Ibid., p. 6.

46. Paul Slovic, Melissa Finucane, Ellen Peters, and Donald G. MacGregor, "The Affect Heuristic," in *Heuristics and Biases: The Psychology of Intuitive Judgment.*

47. Ibid.

48. W. Kip Viscusi and Richard J. Zeckhauser, "Sacrificing Civil Liberties to Reduce Terrorism Risk," January 10, 2003, available at <http://ksghome.harvard.edu/~.RZeckhauser.Academic.Ksg/SCL.pdf>.

49. Melissa L. Finucane, Ali Alhakami, Paul Slovic, and Stephen M. Johnson, "The Affect Heuristic in Judgments of Risks and Benefits," in Paul Slovic, *The Perception of Risk,* pp. 415–16.

50. David A. Dana, *A Behavioral Economic Defense of the Precautionary Principle,* 97 Nw. U.L. Rev. 1315, 1321 (2003).

51. See Robert Hahn, *The Economics of Airline Safety and Security,* 20 Harv. J. L. & Pub. Pol'y. 791, 809 (1997).

52. Ann Cavoukian and Tyler J. Hamilton, *The Privacy Payoff: How Successful Businesses Build Customer Trust* (Toronto: McGraw-Hill Ryerson, 2002), pp. 4–5.

53. Ibid.

54. Ibid., p. 9.

55. Ibid., pp. 256–57.

56. W. Kip Viscusi and Richard J. Zeckhauser, "Sacrificing Civil Liberties to Reduce Terrorism Risk," pp. 11–12.

57. Ann Cavoukian, "Security Technologies Enabling Privacy (STEPs): Time for a Paradigm Shift," June 2002, available at <http://www.ipc.on.ca/scripts/index_.asp?action=31&P_ID=13289&N_ID=1&PT_ID=11351&U_ID=0>.

58. See Esther Dyson, "Blindfolding Big Brother," *The New York Times* Special Features, April 17, 2002.

59. Michael Waidner, "Enabling Trust in e-Business: Research in Enterprise Privacy Technologies," IBM Privacy Research Institute, 2002, available at <http://www.zurich.ibm.com>.

Chapter Three: The Silver Bullet

1. Jennifer 8. Lee, "Federal Agents Look to Adapt Private Technology," *The New York Times*, January 14, 2002, p. C4.

2. White House, Office of Homeland Security, NATIONAL STRATEGY FOR HOMELAND SECURITY (2002), p. 51, available at <http://www.whitehouse.gov/homeland/book/sect4-1/.pdf>.

3. Robert O'Harrow, Jr., "Air Security Focusing on Flier Screening: Complex Profiling Network Months Behind Schedule," *The Washington Post*, September 4, 2002, p. A1.

4. Rex A. Hudson and the staff of the Federal Research Division of the Library of Congress, *Who Becomes a Terrorist and Why: The 1999 Government Report on Profiling Terrorists* (Guilford, Conn.: Lyons Press, 1999), p. 67.

5. Ibid., p. 68.

6. Christopher Guzelian and Mariano-Florentino Cuéllar, *When Terrorists Are the Needles and America Is the Haystack,* unpublished draft on file with the author.

7. Samidh Chakrabarti and Aaron Strauss, "Carnival Booth: An Algorithm for Defeating the Computer-Assisted Passenger Screening System," *First Monday*, vol. 7, no. 10, October 2002, available at <http://firstmonday.org/issues/issue7_10/chakrabarti/#note43>.

8. Larry Ellison, "Digital IDs Can Help Prevent Terrorism," *The Wall Street Journal*, October 8, 2001, p. A26.

9. See, e.g., Dr. George Tomko, "Biometrics as a Privacy-Enhancing Technology: Friend or Foe of Privacy?" address at the Privacy Laws and Business Ninth Privacy Commissioners/Data Protection Authorities Workshop (September 15, 1998), available at <http://www.dss.state.ct.us/digital/tomko.htm>.

10. Ibid.

11. See, e.g., Rakesh Agrawal and Ramakrishnan Srikant, "Privacy-Preserving Data Mining," in PROC. OF THE 2000 ACM-SIGMOD INT'L CONFERENCE ON MANAGEMENT OF DATA, May 2000.

12. *Security with Privacy,* ISAT 2002 Study, December 13, 2002, p. 10, available at <epic.org>.

13. Doug Dyer, address at DARPATech 2002 Conference, August 2002.

14. Charles C. Mann, "Homeland Insecurity," *The Atlantic Monthly,* September 2002, p. 101.

15. Christopher Lasch, *The True and Only Heaven: Progress and Its Critics* (New York: W. W. Norton, 1991), pp. 362–63.

16. Mark J. Barrenchea, *E-Business or Out of Business: Oracle's Roadmap for Profiting in the New Economy* (New York: McGraw-Hill, 2001), pp. 43–44.

17. James B. Rule, *Private Lives and Public Surveillance: Social Control in the Computer Age* (New York: Schocken Books, 1974), p. 28.

Chapter Four: The Path of the Law

1. Randolph S. Bourne, *War and the Intellectuals: Collected Essays, 1915–1919* (New York: Harper and Row, 1964), p. 71.

2. Ibid., p. 70.

3. Ibid., p. 75.

4. For my own fears on this score, see Jeffrey Rosen, "Law and Order: Terrorism and Freedom, Then and Now," *The New Republic,* September 24, 2001, p. 17.

5. Neil A. Lewis, "Ashcroft's Terrorism Policies Dismay Some Conservatives," *The New York Times,* July 24, 2002, p. A1.

6. Sec. 807, Amendments to H.R. 5005, adopted by the Committee on the Judiciary, July 10, 2002.

7. Adam Clymer, "Senate Rejects Pentagon Plan to Mine Citizens' Personal Data for Clues to Terrorism," *The New York Times,* January 24, 2003, p. A12.

8. Richard Hofstadter, *The Paranoid Style in American Politics* (New York: Vintage, 1967), p. 29.

9. Ibid., p. 5.

10. George M. Marsden, *Fundamentalism and American Culture: The Shaping of Twentieth-Century Evangelicalism, 1870–1925* (New York: Oxford University Press, 1980), p. 52.

11. Joel Dyer, *Harvest of Rage: Why Oklahoma City Is Only the Beginning* (Boulder, Co.: Westview Press, 1998), p. 131.

12. See "How the USA PATRIOT Act Puts the CIA Back in the Business of Spying on Americans" (October 23, 2001), available at <http://archive.aclu.org/Congress/L102301j.html>.

13. William Stuntz, *Local Policing after the Terror,* 111 YALE L.J. 2137, 2183–84 (2002).

14. See, e.g., James X. Dempsy, *Communications Privacy in the Digital Age: Revitalizing the Federal Wiretap Laws to Enhance Privacy,* 8 ALB. L.J. SCI. & TECH. 65, 75 (1997).

15. See Orin S. Kerr, *The Fourth Amendment in New Technologies: Constitutional Myths and the Case for Restraint* (unpublished draft on file with the author.)

16. Hamdi v. Rumsfeld, 296 F.3d 278, 283 (4th Cir. 2002).

17. Hamdi v. Rumsfeld, 316 F.3d 450, 473 (4th Cir. 2003).

18. See Center for National Security Studies v. U.S. Dep't of Justice, 2003 U.S. App. LEXIS 1190. See also Thomas F. Powers, "Can We Be Secure and Free?" *The Public Interest,* no. 151, spring 2003, pp. 11–12.

19. Robert G. McCloskey, *The American Supreme Court* (Chicago: University of Chicago Press, 1994), p. 14.

20. See Lucas A. Powe, Jr., *The Warren Court and American Politics* (Cambridge: Harvard University Press, 2000).

21. William Stuntz, *Local Policing after the Terror,* 111 YALE L.J., at p. 2138.

22. See, e.g., Miller v. California, 423 U.S. 15 (1972); Smith v. Maryland, 442 U.S. 735 (1979).

23. Katz v. United States, 389 U.S. 347 (1967).

24. Glenn R. Simpson, "Big Brother-in-Law: If the FBI Hopes to Get

the Goods on You, It May Ask ChoicePoint," *The Wall Street Journal,* April 13, 2001, p. A1.

25. Daniel J. Solove, *Digital Dossiers and the Dissipation of Fourth Amendment Privacy,* 75 S. CAL. L. REV. 1083, 1098 (2002).

26. Atwater v. City of Lago Vista, 532 U.S. 319 (2001).

27. Whren v. United States, 517 U.S. 906 (1996).

28. William Stuntz, *Local Policing after the Terror,* 111 YALE L.J., at 2158.

29. See Thomas Y. Davies, *The Fictional Character of Law-and-Order Originalism: A Case Study of the Distortions and Evasions of Framing-Era Arrest Doctrine in* Atwater v. Lago Vista, 37 WAKE FOREST L. REV. 239, 246 (2002).

30. Paul v. Davis, 424 U.S. 693, 699 (1976).

31. Smith v. Doe, 123 S. Ct. 1140 (2003) (Ginsburg, J., dissenting).

32. Doe v. Dep't of Pub. Safety, 271 F.3d 38, 47 (2nd Cir. 2001), *rev'd sub nom.* Conn. Dep't of Public Safety v. Doe, 123 S.Ct. 1160 (2003).

33. See, e.g., United States v. Weaver, 966 F.2d 391 (8th Cir. 1992).

Chapter Five: Identity Crisis

1. Janny Scott, "Closing a Scrapbook Full of Life and Sorrow," *The New York Times,* December 31, 2001, p. B6.

2. Ibid.

3. Thomas Mallon, "The Mourning Paper," *The American Scholar,* spring 2002, pp. 6–7.

4. "The Victims: Portraits of Grief: 'Stanley McCaskill: Proud to Be a Mama's Boy,' " *The New York Times,* September 15, 2002, p. A11.

5. Anthony Giddens and Christopher Pierson, *Conversations with Anthony Giddens: Making Sense of Modernity* (Stanford: Stanford University Press, 1998), p. 101.

6. Erich Fromm, *The Sane Society* (New York: Reinhart, 1955), pp. 141–42.

7. Charles Derber, *The Pursuit of Attention: Power and Ego in Everyday Life* (New York: Oxford University Press, 2000), p. 81.

8. Daniel J. Boorstin, *The Image: A Guide to Pseudo-Events in America* (New York: Atheneum, 1977), p. 193.

9. See "Online Diary: Blog Nation," *The New York Times,* August 22, 2002, p. E3.

10. <http://www.dooce.com/about.html>.

11. Alexis de Tocqueville, *Democracy in America,* eds. Harvey C. Mansfield and Delba Winthrop, vol. 2, part 2, ch. 13 (Chicago: University of Chicago Press, 2000), p. 513.

12. See generally Lawrence M. Friedman, *The Horizontal Society* (New Haven: Yale University Press, 1999).

13. Kenneth S. Greenberg, *Honor & Slavery* (Princeton: Princeton University Press, 1996), p. 22.

14. Karen Halttunen, *Confidence Men and Painted Women: A Study of Middle-Class Culture in America, 1830–1870* (New Haven: Yale University Press, 1982), p. 6.

15. Ibid., pp. 6–7.

16. Ibid., p. 54.

17. Lionel Trilling, *Sincerity and Authenticity* (Cambridge: Harvard University Press, 1972).

18. Peter L. Berger, Brigitte Berger, and Hansfried Kellner, *The Homeless Mind: Modernization and Consciousness* (New York: Random House, 1973), p. 90.

19. Richard Sennett, *The Fall of Public Man* (New York: W. W. Norton, 1974), p. 196.

20. Ibid., p. 265.

21. Daniel J. Boorstin, *The Image,* p. 57.

22. Ibid., pp. 57–58.

23. David McNally and Karl D. Speak, *Be Your Own Brand: A Breakthrough Formula for Standing Out from the Crowd* (San Francisco: Berrett-Koehler, 2002), p. 4.

24. Ibid., pp. 7, 11.
25. Ibid., p.13.
26. Ibid., p. 22.
27. Ibid., p. 13.
28. Ibid., p. 67.
29. Ibid., p. 47.
30. Alex Kuczynski, "Hold Me! Squeeze Me! Buy a 6-Pack!" *The New York Times,* November 16, 1997, Sunday Styles, sec. 9, p. 1.
31. See Ruth Shalit, "The Inner Doughboy," Salon.com, March 23, 2000, available at <http://archive.salon.com/media/col/shal/2000/03/23/doughboy>.
32. Daniel J. Boorstin, *The Image,* p. 198.
33. John Stuart Mill, "On Liberty," in *On Liberty and Other Essays* (New York: Oxford University Press, 1998), p. 82.
34. Ibid., pp. 79, 82.
35. Joshua Meyrowitz, *No Sense of Place: The Impact of Electronic Media on Social Behavior* (New York: Oxford University Press, 1985), p. 6.
36. Roxane Cohen Silver, E. Alison Holman, Daniel N. McIntosh, Michael Poulin, and Virginia Gil-Rivas, *Nationwide Longitudinal Study of Psychological Responses to September 11,* 288 JAMA 1235, 1241–42 (2002).
37. J. W. Pennebaker and A. Graybeal, "Patterns of Natural Language Use: Disclosure, Personality, and Social Integration," 10 CURRENT DIRECTIONS IN PSYCHOLOGICAL SCIENCE 92 (2001).
38. Richard Sennett, *The Fall of Public Man,* p. 262.
39. John Stuart Mill, "The Subjection of Women," in *On Liberty and Other Essays* (New York: Oxford University Press, 1998), p. 575.
40. Anthony Giddens, *Modernity and Self-Identity: Self and Society in the Late Modern Age* (Stanford: Stanford University Press, 1991), p. 94.
41. *Lord Chesterfield's Letters* (Oxford: Oxford University Press, 1998), p. 174.

42. Milan Kundera, *The Book of Laughter and Forgetting* (New York: Perennial Classics, 1999), pp. 127–28.
43. Ibid., p. 146.
44. Ibid., p. 147.
45. Charles Derber, *The Pursuit of Attention*, pp. xv–xviii.

Epilogue: An Escape from Fear

1. David Brin, *The Transparent Society: Will Technology Force Us to Choose between Privacy and Freedom?* (Reading: Perseus, 1998), p. 9.
2. Ibid., p. 4.
3. Ibid., p. 282.
4. Ibid., p. 5.
5. Brandon C. Welsh and David P. Farrington, *Crime Prevention Effects of Closed Circuit Television: A Systematic Review,* Home Office Research Study 252, August 2002, pp. 10–11, available at <http://www.homeoffice.gov.uk/rds/pdfs2/hors252.pdf>.
6. David Brin, *The Transparent Society,* pp. 334–35.
7. *Lord Chesterfield's Letters* (Oxford: Oxford University Press, 1998), p. 54.
8. Rogers Worthington, "A Family Tragedy or Terrorists' Scheme?" *The Chicago Tribune,* June 13, 1993, p. C21.
9. United States v. Isa, 923 F.2d 1300, 1304 (1991).
10. Id., at 1305 (citing United States v. Hawamda, no. 89–56–A, slip op. [E.D. Va., April 17, 1989]); see also United States v. Pelton, 835 F.2d 1067, 1075–76 (4th Cir. 1987); United States v. Cavanagh, 807 F.2d 787, 790–91 (9th Cir. 1987); United States v. Badia, 827 F.2d 1458, 1464 (11th Cir. 1987); United States v. Duggan, 743 F.2d 59, 78 (2nd Cir. 1984); United States v. Belfield, 692 F.2d 141, 147–49 (D.C. Cir. 1982).
11. In Re: Sealed Case, 310 F.3d 717, 724 (Foreign Int. 2002).
12. Ibid., at 736.

13. Craig M. Bradley, *The Exclusionary Rule in Germany*, 96 HARV. L. REV. 1032, 1054–55 (1983).

14. See Perez v. Sharp, 32 Cal. 2d 711 (1948) and Loving v. Virginia, 388 U.S. 1 (1967).

15. Herma Hill Kay, *From the Second Sex to the Joint Venture: An Overview of Women's Rights and Family Law in the United States during the Twentieth Century*, 88 CAL. L. REV. 2017, 2037 and n. 117 (2000), citing Somini Sengupta, "Marry at Will," *The New York Times*, November 12, 2000, p. WR2.

16. See Olmstead v. United States, 277 U.S. 438 (1928) and Katz v. United States, 389 U.S. 347, 351 (1967).

17. United States v. White, 401 U.S. 745, 786 (1971) (Harlan, J., dissenting).

18. Ibid., at 796–97.

19. Opinion by Justice Gérard V. La Forest on Video Surveillance, April 5, 2002, available at <http://www.privcom.gc.ca/media/nr-c/opinion_020410_e.asp>.

20. Id. See also Anthony Amsterdam, *Perspectives on the Fourth Amendment*, 58 MINN. L. REV. 349, 403 (1974).

21. United States v. White, 401 U.S. at 786 (Harlan, J., dissenting).

22. City of Indianapolis v. Edmond, 531 U.S. 32, 44 (2000).

23. Re: Opinion—CCRA Passenger Name Record, opinion by retired Supreme Court Justice Hon. Gérard V. La Forest, November 19, 2002, available at <http://www.privcom.gc.ca/media/nr-c/opinion_021122_lf_e.asp>.

24. Craig M. Bradley, *The Exclusionary Rule in Germany*, 96 HARV. L. REV., at 1041.

25. Ibid., n. 43, citing *Judgment of June 10, 1963*, BVerfG, 16 BVerfG 194.

26. Ibid., at 1042–43, n. 48, citing *The Diary Case*, judgment of February 21, 1964, BGH, 19 BGHSt 325.

27. John Wadham, *Human Rights and Privacy—the Balance* (March

2000), reprinted in Daniel J. Solove and Marc Rotenberg, *Information Privacy Law* (New York: Aspen, 2003), p. 693.

28. P. G. and J. H. v. United Kingdom, ECHR, September 25, 2001, reprinted in Daniel J. Solove and Marc Rotenberg, *Information Privacy Law,* p. 698.

29. Rotaru v. Romania, ECHR, May 4, 2000, reprinted in Daniel J. Solove and Marc Rotenberg, *Information Privacy Law,* p. 706.

30. See, e.g., George Radwanski, testimony regarding Bill C–36, the Anti-Terrorism Act, to the House of Commons Standing Committee on Justice and Human Rights (October 23, 2001), available at <http://www.privcom.gc.ca/speech/02_05_a_011024_e.asp>.

31. See letter from George Radwanski to Minister Lawrence MacAulay, the solicitor general (May 17, 2002), available at <www.privcom.gc.ca/media/an/ac_020517_e.asp>.

32. See fact sheet, Canada Customs and Revenue Agency, "Advance Passenger Information/Passenger Name Record (API/PNR)" (October 2002), available at <www.ccra-adrc.gc.ca/newsroom/fact sheets/2002/oct/api-e.html>.

33. Priscilla M. Regan, *Legislating Privacy: Technology, Social Values, and Public Policy* (Chapel Hill: University of North Carolina Press, 1995), p. 80.

34. Ibid., p. 175.

35. Ibid., p. 177.

36. Ibid., p. 178.

37. Ibid.

38. See Amitai Etzioni and Deidre Mead, "The State of Society— a Rush to Pre-9/11," available at <http://www.gwu.edu/~ccps/The_State_of_Society.html>.

39. Julia Scheeres, "Support for ID Cards Waning," Wired.com, March 13, 2002, available at <http://www.wired.com/news/print/0,1294,51000,00.html>.

40. Paul Slovic, "Perception of Risk from Radiation," in Paul Slovic, *The Perception of Risk* (Sterling, Va.: Earthscan, 2000), p. 271.

41. Ibid., p. 268.

42. Ibid., p. 272.

43. Ibid., p. 269.

44. Baruch Fischoff, "Assessing and Communicating the Risks of Terrorism," remarks delivered at the 27th Annual AAAS Colloquium on Science and Technology Policy, April 11–12, 2002.

45. Anthony Giddens and Christopher Pierson, *Conversations with Anthony Giddens: Making Sense of Modernity* (Stanford: Stanford University Press, 1998), p. 212.

46. Paul Slovic, "Perceived Risk, Trust and Democracy" in Paul Slovic, *The Perception of Risk,* pp. 324–25.

47. Franklin D. Roosevelt, First Inaugural Address, March 4, 1933, reprinted in *The Public Papers and Addresses of Franklin D. Roosevelt,* ed. Samuel I. Rosenman (New York: Random House, 1938), p. 11.

48. John G. Nicolay and John Hay, eds., *Complete Works of Abraham Lincoln,* vol. 1 (New York: Lamb Publishing Company, 1904), pp. 35–50.

Index

ABOUT THE AUTHOR

JEFFREY ROSEN is a law professor at George Washington University and the legal affairs editor of *The New Republic.* His essays and commentaries have appeared in many publications, including *The New York Times Magazine* and *The New Yorker,* and on National Public Radio. Rosen is a graduate of Harvard College, Oxford University, and Yale Law School. He lives in Washington, D.C.

This bo
signed l
pher Ja
design i
of Clau
cally to
type fo
Monot
the far
Sabon,

4/04